RAND

The Demographic Dividend

A New Perspective on the Economic Consequences of Population Change

David E. Bloom
David Canning
Jaypee Sevilla

Supported by the
William and Flora Hewlett Foundation
David and Lucile Packard Foundation
Rockefeller Foundation
United Nations Population Fund

POPULATION MATTERS

A RAND Program of Policy-Relevant Research Communication

The research described in this report was supported by the William and Flora Hewlett Foundation, the David and Lucile Packard Foundation, the Rockefeller Foundation, and the United Nations Population Fund.

Library of Congress Cataloging-in-Publication Data

Bloom, David E.
    The demographic dividend : a new perspective on the economic consequences of population change / David E. Bloom, David Canning, Jaypee Sevilla.
        p. cm.
    "MR-1274."
    ISBN 0-8330-2926-6
    1. Demographic transition. 2. Age distribution (Demography) 3. Population. 4. Fertility, Human. 5. Economic development. 6. Demographic transition—Developing countries. I. Canning, David. II. Sevilla, Jaypee. III.Title.

HB887 .B58 2002
304.6'2—dc21

                                                                        2002024818

Published 2003 by RAND
1700 Main Street, P.O. Box 2138, Santa Monica, CA 90407-2138
1200 South Hayes Street, Arlington, VA 22202-5050
201 North Craig Street, Suite 202, Pittsburgh, PA 15213-1516
RAND URL: http://www.rand.org/
To order RAND documents or to obtain additional information, contact Distribution Services: Telephone: (310) 451-7002;
Fax: (310) 451-6915; Email: order@rand.org

How does population growth affect economic development? Economists, demographers, and policymakers have debated this question for decades. Various studies have suggested that population growth can be detrimental to economic development, or beneficial, depending on circumstances. More recently, the neutralist view that rapid population growth neither promotes nor impedes economic growth has held sway. The emergence of this view has coincided with a declining interest in family planning as an instrument of economic development. The latest evidence suggests, however, that the debate may have been framed too narrowly. It has focused almost exclusively on population size and growth rates. Little attention has been paid to a critical variable: the age structure of the population (that is, the way in which the population is distributed across different age groups). Taking account of age structure provides powerful confirmation of the age-old view that, when it comes to the determination of living standards, population does, indeed, matter.

This report reviews the debate over the effects of demographic change on economic growth and examines the research evidence on the economic impact of changes in age structure. It also examines the relationship between population change and economic development in particular regions of the world, including East Asia, Latin America, sub-Saharan Africa, and the Middle East and North Africa. Finally, it discusses how changes in the age structure interact with labor-market, health, and education policies to contribute to economic growth.

Understanding the relationship between population change and economic growth has taken on added importance in recent years because the world's developing countries—home to the vast majority of the world's population—are in varying stages of a demographic transition from high to low rates of mortality and fertility. This transition produces a "boom" generation that is gradually working its way through each nation's age structure. As the boom generation enters working age, there is the opportunity to unleash an economic growth spurt, provided the right kinds of policies are in place to ensure the extra workers are productively employed. For this reason, policymakers should benefit from a clearer understanding of the relationship between economic development and the changes in age structure that result from the unfolding demographic transition.

This research was conducted for *Population Matters*, a RAND project whose goal is to synthesize and communicate the policy-relevant results of demographic research. Through publications and outreach activities, the project aims to raise awareness and highlight the importance of population policy issues and to provide a scientific basis for public debate over population policy questions. *Population Matters* is part of RAND's Labor and Population Program.

This report has been funded by grants from the William and Flora Hewlett Foundation, the David and Lucile Packard Foundation, the Rockefeller Foundation, and the United Nations Population Fund. For further information and access to other *Population Matters* publications, visit www.rand.org/labor/popmatters. For a complete list of *Population Matters* publications, please see the inside back cover.

CONTENTS

FIGURES

TABLES

DEMOGRAPHIC CHANGE AND ECONOMIC GROWTH: THE IMPORTANCE OF AGE STRUCTURE

For decades, economists and social thinkers have debated the influence of population change on economic growth. Three alternative positions define this debate: Population growth either (1) restricts, (2) promotes, or (3) is independent of economic growth. Proponents of each explanation can find evidence to support their cases. All of these explanations, however, focus on population size and population growth. In recent years, however, the debate has given insufficient attention to a critical issue: the *age structure* of the population (that is, the way in which the population is distributed across different age groups), which can change dramatically as fertility and mortality rates change.

Because people's economic behavior and needs vary at different stages of life, changes in a country's age structure can have significant effects on its economic performance. Nations with a high proportion of children are likely to devote a high proportion of resources to their care, which tends to depress the pace of economic growth. By contrast, if most of a nation's population falls within the working ages, the added productivity of this group can produce a "demographic dividend" of economic growth, assuming that policies to take advantage of this are in place. In fact, the combined effect of this large working-age population and health, family, labor, financial, and human capital policies can effect virtuous cycles of wealth creation. And if a large proportion of a nation's population consists of the elderly, the effects can be similar to those of a very young population. A large share of resources is needed by a relatively less productive segment of the population, which likewise can inhibit economic growth.

After tracing the history of theories of the effects of population growth, this report reviews evidence on the relevance of changes in age structure for economic growth. It also examines the relationship between population change and economic development in particular regions of the world: East Asia; Japan; North America, Western Europe, Australia, and New Zealand; South Central and Southeast Asia; Latin America; the Middle East and North Africa; sub-Saharan Africa; and Eastern Europe and the former Soviet Union. Finally, it discusses the key policy variables that, combined with reduced fertility and increases in the working-age population, have contributed to economic growth in some areas of the developing world.[1]

THE DEMOGRAPHIC TRANSITION AND THE "DEMOGRAPHIC DIVIDEND"

The relationship between population change and economic growth has taken on added salience in recent years because of demographic trends in the developing world. At varying rates and times since World War II, developing countries have been undergoing a demographic transition, from high to low rates of mortality and fertility. This transition is producing a "boom" generation—a generation that is larger than those immediately before and after it—that is gradually working its way through nations' age structures. The East Asian nations were at the forefront of this transition; other regions, including Latin America, began their transitions later, in the 1960s and '70s. Yet

---

[1]The text, tables, and figures for this paper draw heavily on data from a recent CD-ROM published by the United Nations (United Nations, 2001). Unless otherwise noted, we use the UN's "medium variant" for all data. The UN's methodology has been criticized for its reliance on the assumption that all countries will converge to a fertility rate of 2.1 children per woman. The concern here is that this suggests fertility will rise in quite a few countries where the total fertility rate is currently below the replacement level of 2.1. Regardless of the merits of this critique, we note that most of the results presented in this paper are qualitatively insensitive to the difference between the "medium-" and "low-fertility" variants of the data.

other areas—notably some countries in the Middle East and Africa—have not yet fully begun, or are in the early phases of this transition.

THE ESSENTIAL POLICY ENVIRONMENT

Nations undergoing this transition have an opportunity to capitalize on the demographic dividend offered by the maturing of formerly young populations. The demographic dividend is not, however, automatic. Given the right kind of policy environment, this demographic dividend can help to produce a sustained period of economic growth, as it did in several East Asian economies. The critical policy areas include

- public health
- family planning
- education
- economic policies that promote labor-market flexibility, openness to trade, and savings

Policymakers in developing countries have a window of opportunity for exploiting the maturation of previously young populations. Policymakers should consider how to maximize and capture this dividend by accelerating the demographic transition, and allowing extra labor to be absorbed productively in the market. Finally, policymakers must plan for the future health care and pension-income needs of this baby-boom generation when it ages. The demographic transition offers policymakers a window of opportunity. Seizing it could prove vital to the economic and social development of their countries.

Note that policies that enhance the free operation of markets are frequently referred to throughout the report. In most simple economic models, such policies will tend to promote a country's ability to take advantage of the demographic dividend. However, two caveats are in order.

First, policy reforms that make labor markets more flexible are not unambiguously beneficial, especially in the short run. Political feasibility can also be an issue. Although social protection programs can, in principle, ease the impact of labor market reforms, workers who suffer pay reductions, who are displaced, or who fear these outcomes can be a potent political force resisting change. Furthermore, capture of the potential demographic dividend can be impeded by labor market rigidities that pervade many developing countries. These include rules governing the hiring and firing of individuals that prevent employers from taking risks and thus deter investment; minimum wages that exceed market rates and thereby discourage hiring and training; government pay practices that are grossly out of line with the market; and labor market inertia caused by labor-management bargaining.

Second, similar issues arise with respect to free trade, since it is well established that trade liberalization creates both winners and losers. Openness to trade can provoke economic adjustments that lead to unemployment and poverty. There are also some important issues about the fundamental fairness of outcomes that result when countries become more integrated into the world economy. These questions relate, for example, to intellectual property rights, immigration restrictions, and developed country protectionism.

Devising economically and politically realistic programs to deal with these challenges is hugely important, though beyond the scope of this report.

ACKNOWLEDGMENTS

The authors are indebted to Dave Adamson, Nancy Birdsall, Barry Bloom, Dean Jamison, Allen Kelley, Thomas Lindh, Michael Lipton, Pia Malaney, Bo Malmberg, Andrew Mason, Tom Merrick, Larry Rosenberg, Jeffrey Sachs, Stephen Sinding, and Jeffrey Williamson for helpful discussions, and to Julie DaVanzo for detailed written comments on this paper. The authors give special thanks to Steve Baeck, River Path Associates, and Larry Rosenberg for editorial and computational assistance. Earlier versions of this paper have been presented at the World Bank; Brown University; the Aga Khan University; the Yale School of Public Health; the Yale School of Management; the Pan American Health Organization; the Rockefeller Foundation; Harvard University; the Swedish International Development Agency; University of Uppsala; University of Dublin; the Economic History Association; the World Health Organization; the Asian Development Bank; the Inter-American Development Bank; USAID; Centro de Investigación y Docencia Económicas, or CIDE (Mexico); Di Tella University; and Universidad Argentina de la Empresa, or UADE (Argentina).

FDI	foreign direct investment
GDP	gross domestic product
MENA	Middle East and North Africa
NAS	U.S. National Academy of Sciences
UN	United Nations
WHO	World Health Organization

Chapter One

THE DEBATE OVER THE EFFECTS OF POPULATION GROWTH ON ECONOMIC GROWTH

The relationship between population change and economic growth remains a subject of debate among economists and demographers. They continue to disagree about whether population growth (a) restricts, (b) promotes, or (c) is independent of economic growth. Proponents of each view can point to research evidence to support their cases.

The utility of this debate has been hampered by its almost exclusive focus on population *size* and *growth*. Little attention has been paid to a critical variable: the *age structure* of the population (that is, the way in which the population is distributed across different age groups) and how it changes when populations grow.

This report attempts to address this limitation. It reviews the debate over the effects of demographic change on economic growth and examines the evidence for the relevance of changes in age structure for economic growth. It also examines the relationship between population change and economic development in particular regions of the world. Finally, it discusses key policies that, combined with reduced fertility and increases in the working-age population, have contributed to economic growth in the developing world.

Understanding the relationship between population change and economic growth has taken on immense significance in recent years because of demographic trends in the developing world. The world's developing countries—home to the vast majority of the world's population—are in varying stages of a demographic transition from high to low rates of mortality and fertility. This transition is producing a boom generation that is gradually working its way through nations' age structures. In conjunction with the right kinds of policies, this phenomenon creates opportunities for economic growth in developing countries. For this reason, policymakers should benefit from a clearer understanding of the relationship between economic development and the shifting age structure that results from the unfolding demographic transition.

THE "PESSIMISTIC" THEORY: POPULATION GROWTH RESTRICTS ECONOMIC GROWTH

After World War II, rapid population growth, resulting from the gap between declining mortality and continuing high fertility, began occurring in much of Asia. By the mid-1960s, more countries, including a number in Latin America and the Middle East, were experiencing unprecedented rates of population growth. At such rates, their populations would double in less than 25 years.

Concerns about rapid population growth voiced by demographers, social scientists, and others were based largely on the assumption that such growth would "serve as a brake" on economic development.[1] In the late 1940s, conservationists began to write about excessive population growth as a threat to food supplies and natural resources. Concerns about the impact of rapid population growth and high fertility motivated the widespread implementation of family planning programs in many areas of the developing world (see Seltzer, 2002). Policymakers presumed that by helping to reduce high fertility, family planning programs would slow population growth, which in turn would contribute to improved economic performance by freeing resources that otherwise would be devoted to child-rearing and by reducing strains on infrastructure and the environment.

The "pessimistic" theory traces its lineage to Thomas Malthus. Writing in the 1790s, Malthus asked whether "the future improvement of

---

[1]For one interesting discussion of trends in global population growth since the 1950s and the development implications of family planning, see Bulatao (1998), pp. 3–20.

society" was possible in the face of ever larger populations. He reached his famously dismal conclusion:

> "Taking the population of the world at any number, a thousand millions, for instance ... the human species would increase in the ratio of 1, 2, 4, 8, 16, 32, 64, 128, 256, 516, etc. and subsistence as 1, 2, 3, 4, 5, 6, 7, 8, 9, 10, etc. In two centuries and a quarter the population would be to the means of subsistence as 512 to 10; in three centuries as 4096 to 13, and in two thousand years the difference would be incalculable"(Malthus, 1798).

In a world with fixed resources for growing food, and slow technical progress, Malthus theorized, food production would quickly be swamped by the pressures of a rapidly growing population. The available diet would then fall below subsistence level, until population growth was halted by a high death rate. Living standards could only ever improve in the short term—before they set in motion more rapid population growth. The balance between population and income growth was the "great law of our nature." Accordingly,

> "No fancied equality, no agrarian regulations in their utmost extent, could remove the pressure of it even for a single century. And it appears, therefore, to be decisive against the possible existence of a society, all the members of which should live in ease, happiness, and comparative leisure; and feel no anxiety about providing the means of subsistence for themselves and families"(Malthus, 1798).

Malthus's pessimism has remained with us. In 1968, for instance, Paul Ehrlich opened his influential book *The Population Bomb* with the words, "The battle ... is over. In the 1970s hundreds of millions of people are going to starve to death"(Ehrlich, 1968). More measured studies undertaken by the U.S. National Academy of Sciences (NAS) in 1971 and the United Nations in 1973 also predicted that the net effect of population growth would be negative (National Academy of Sciences, 1971; United Nations, 1973). Rapid population growth continues to press on the modern consciousness. The world's population has grown sixfold since 1800, when it stood at about 1 billion. It took less than 130 years to add another billion. Things have quickened considerably since. The 6 billionth baby was born in October 1999—and world population is forecast to reach 9.3 billion by the year 2050 (see Table 1.1). Table 1.2 shows the current population

Table 1.1

World Population in Billions, 1804–2043

1 billion in 1804
2 billion in 1927 (123 years later)
3 billion in 1960 (33 years later)
4 billion in 1974 (14 years later)
5 billion in 1987 (13 years later)
6 billion in 1999 (12 years later)
7 billion in 2012 (13 years later)
8 billion in 2026 (14 years later)
9 billion in 2043 (17 years later)

SOURCES: Population Division, Department of Economic and Social Affairs, UN Secretariat, *Population Newsletter*, No. 66, December 1998; and United Nations (2001).

Table 1.2

Total Population in 2001, by Region, Subregion, and Country (Thousands)

Area, Region, Subregion, or Country	Population	Share of World Population
WORLD	6,134,135	
More-developed regions[a]	1,193,861	19.5%
Less-developed regions[b]	4,940,274	80.5%
Least-developed countries[c]	674,954	11.0%

[a]United Nations (2001) defines *more-developed regions* as "all regions of Europe plus Northern America, Australia/New Zealand and Japan."

[b]United Nations (2001) defines *less-developed regions* as "all regions of Africa, Asia (excluding Japan), Latin America and the Caribbean plus Melanesia, Micronesia and Polynesia."

[c]United Nations (2001) follows the United Nations General Assembly's 1998 definition of *least-developed countries* as these 48 countries: Afghanistan, Angola, Bangladesh, Benin, Bhutan, Burkina Faso, Burundi, Cambodia, Cape Verde, Central African Republic, Chad, Comoros, Democratic Republic of the Congo, Djibouti, Equatorial Guinea, Eritrea, Ethiopia, Gambia, Guinea, Guinea-Bissau, Haiti, Kiribati, Lao People's Democratic Republic, Lesotho, Liberia, Madagascar, Malawi, Maldives, Mali, Mauritania, Mozambique, Myanmar, Nepal, Niger, Rwanda, Samoa, São Tomé and Príncipe, Sierra Leone, Solomon Islands, Somalia, Sudan, Togo, Tuvalu, Uganda, United Republic of Tanzania, Vanuatu, Yemen and Zambia. These countries are also included in the less-developed regions, except where otherwise stated.

Table 1.2—continued

Area, Region, Subregion, or Country	Population	Share of World Population
AFRICA	812,603	13.2%
Eastern Africa	256,673	4.2%
Burundi	6,502	
Comoros	727	
Djibouti	644	
Eritrea	3,816	
Ethiopia	64,459	
Kenya	31,293	
Madagascar	16,437	
Malawi	11,572	
Mauritius	1,171	
Mozambique	18,644	
Réunion	732	
Rwanda	7,949	
Seychelles	81	
Somalia	9,157	
Uganda	24,023	
United Republic of Tanzania	35,965	
Zambia	10,649	
Zimbabwe	12,852	
Middle Africa	98,151	1.6%
Angola	13,527	
Cameroon	15,203	
Central African Republic	3,782	
Chad	8,135	
Congo	3,110	
Democratic Republic of the Congo	52,522	
Equatorial Guinea	470	
Gabon	1,262	
São Tomé and Príncipe	140	
Northern Africa	177,391	2.9%
Algeria	30,841	
Egypt	69,080	
Libyan Arab Jamahiriya	5,408	
Morocco	30,430	
Sudan	31,809	
Tunisia	9,562	
Western Sahara	260	

Table 1.2—continued

Area, Region, Subregion, or Country	Population	Share of World Population
Southern Africa	50,129	0.8%
Botswana	1,554	
Lesotho	2,057	
Namibia	1,788	
South Africa	43,792	
Swaziland	938	
Western Africa	230,259	3.8%
Benin	6,446	
Burkina Faso	11,856	
Cape Verde	437	
Côte d'Ivoire	16,349	
Gambia	1,337	
Ghana	19,734	
Guinea	8,274	
Guinea Bissau	1,227	
Liberia	3,108	
Mali	11,677	
Mauritania	2,747	
Niger	11,227	
Nigeria	116,929	
Saint Helena	6	
Senegal	9,662	
Sierra Leone	4,587	
Togo	4,657	
ASIA	3,720,705	60.7%
East Asia	1,491,772	24.3%
China	1,284,972	
China, Hong Kong SAR (Special Administrative Area)	6,961	
China, Macao SAR (Special Administrative Area)	449	
Dem. People's Republic of Korea	22,428	
Japan	127,335	
Mongolia	2,559	
Republic of Korea	47,069	

Table 1.2—continued

Area, Region, Subregion, or Country	Population	Share of World Population
South Central Asia	1,506,727	24.6%
Afghanistan	22,474	
Bangladesh	140,369	
Bhutan	2,141	
India	1,025,096	
Iran (Islamic Republic of)	71,369	
Kazakhstan	16,095	
Kyrgyzstan	4,986	
Maldives	300	
Nepal	23,593	
Pakistan	144,971	
Sri Lanka	19,104	
Tajikistan	6,135	
Turkmenistan	4,835	
Uzbekistan	25,257	
Southeast Asia	529,762	8.6%
Brunei Darussalam	335	
Cambodia	13,441	
East Timor	750	
Indonesia	214,840	
Lao People's Democratic Republic	5,403	
Malaysia	22,633	
Myanmar	48,364	
Philippines	77,131	
Singapore	4,108	
Thailand	63,584	
Viet Nam	79,175	

Table 1.2—continued

Area, Region, Subregion, or Country	Population	Share of World Population
Western Asia	**192,445**	**3.1%**
Armenia	3,788	
Azerbaijan	8,096	
Bahrain	652	
Cyprus	790	
Georgia	5,239	
Iraq	23,584	
Israel	6,172	
Jordan	5,051	
Kuwait	1,971	
Lebanon	3,556	
Occupied Palestinian Territory	3,311	
Oman	2,622	
Qatar	575	
Saudi Arabia	21,028	
Syrian Arab Republic	16,610	
Turkey	67,632	
United Arab Emirates	2,654	
Yemen	19,114	
EUROPE	**726,312**	**11.8%**
Eastern Europe	**302,619**	**4.9%**
Belarus	10,147	
Bulgaria	7,867	
Czech Republic	10,260	
Hungary	9,917	
Poland	38,577	
Republic of Moldova	4,285	
Romania	22,388	
Russian Federation	144,664	
Slovakia	5,403	
Ukraine	49,112	

Table 1.2—continued

Area, Region, Subregion, or Country	Population	Share of World Population
Northern Europe	95,236	1.6%
Channel Islands	145	
Denmark	5,333	
Estonia	1,377	
Faeroe Islands	47	
Finland	5,178	
Iceland	281	
Ireland	3,841	
Isle of Man	76	
Latvia	2,406	
Lithuania	3,689	
Norway	4,488	
Sweden	8,833	
United Kingdom	59,542	
Southern Europe	145,050	2.4%
Albania	3,145	
Andorra	90	
Bosnia and Herzegovina	4,067	
Croatia	4,655	
Gibraltar	27	
Greece	10,623	
Holy See	1	
Italy	57,503	
Malta	392	
Portugal	10,033	
San Marino	27	
Slovenia	1,985	
Spain	39,921	
TFYR Macedonia	2,044	
Yugoslavia	10,538	
Western Europe	183,407	3.0%
Austria	8,075	
Belgium	10,264	
France	59,453	
Germany	82,007	
Liechtenstein	33	
Luxembourg	442	
Monaco	34	
Netherlands	15,930	
Switzerland	7,170	

Table 1.2—continued

Area, Region, Subregion, or Country	Population	Share of World Population
LATIN AMERICA AND THE CARIBBEAN	526,533	8.6%
Caribbean	38,329	0.6%
Anguilla	12	
Antigua and Barbuda	65	
Aruba	104	
Bahamas	308	
Barbados	268	
British Virgin Islands	24	
Cayman Islands	40	
Cuba	11,237	
Dominica	71	
Dominican Republic	8,507	
Grenada	94	
Guadeloupe	431	
Haiti	8,270	
Jamaica	2,598	
Martinique	386	
Montserrat	3	
Netherlands Antilles	217	
Puerto Rico	3,952	
Saint Kitts and Nevis	38	
Saint Lucia	149	
Saint Vincent and the Grenadines	114	
Trinidad and Tobago	1,300	
Turks and Caicos Islands	17	
United States Virgin Islands	122	
Central America	137,480	2.2%
Belize	231	
Costa Rica	4,112	
El Salvador	6,400	
Guatemala	11,687	
Honduras	6,575	
Mexico	100,368	
Nicaragua	5,208	
Panama	2,899	

Table 1.2—continued

Area, Region, Subregion, or Country	Population	Share of World Population
South America	350,724	5.7%
Argentina	37,488	
Bolivia	8,516	
Brazil	172,559	
Chile	15,402	
Colombia	42,803	
Ecuador	12,880	
Falkland Islands (Malvinas)	2	
French Guiana	170	
Guyana	763	
Paraguay	5,636	
Peru	26,093	
Suriname	419	
Uruguay	3,361	
Venezuela	24,632	
NORTHERN AMERICA	317,068	5.2%
Bermuda	63	
Canada	31,015	
Greenland	56	
Saint Pierre et Miquelon	7	
United States of America	285,926	
OCEANIA	30,915	0.5%
Australia/New Zealand	23,146	0.4%
Australia	19,338	
New Zealand	3,808	
Melanesia	6,627	0.1%
Fiji	823	
New Caledonia	220	
Papua New Guinea	4,920	
Solomon Islands	463	
Vanuatu	202	
Micronesia	528	0.0%
Guam	158	
Kiribati	84	
Marshall Islands	52	
Micronesia (Federated States of)	126	
Nauru	13	
Northern Mariana Islands	76	
Palau	20	

Table 1.2—continued

Area, Region, Subregion, or Country	Population	Share of World Population
Polynesia	613	0.0%
American Samoa	70	
Cook Islands	20	
French Polynesia	237	
Niue	2	
Pitcairn	0	
Samoa	159	
Tokelau	1	
Tonga	99	
Tuvalu	10	
Wallis and Futuna Islands	15	
Less-developed regions excluding China	3,647,893	59.5%
Less-developed regions excluding the least developed countries	4,265,320	69.5%
Sub-Saharan Africa	667,022	10.9%

SOURCE: United Nations, "World Population Prospects: The 2000 Revision," CD-ROM, 2001.

of all regions and countries, along with the share of the world's total population in each region. With the population of many developed countries decreasing by 2050, all of this explosive population growth is happening in developing countries (United Nations, 2001) (see Figure 1.1)—most rapidly in those geographic regions that are most fragile and least hospitable (due to adverse climate, lack of resources, or unfavorable location) to economic growth (Sachs, Mellinger, and Gallup, 2001)—encouraging predictions of demographic catastrophe.

For a time, it seemed the pessimists had the right answer. Innovations in agriculture, such as irrigation in China and potato cultivation in Ireland, were accompanied by vast increases in population that hampered improvements in living standards. Until 1700, income gaps between countries were fairly small and, even in 1820, real income levels in the advanced European nations were only about two to three times those found in Africa, Asia, and Latin America (see Figure 1.2).

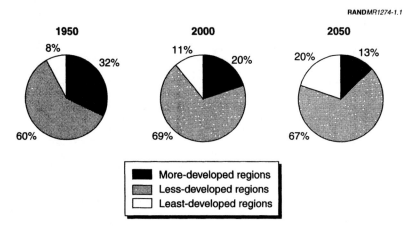

RANDMR1274-1.1

SOURCE: United Nations, "World Population Prospects: The 2000 Revision,"
CD-ROM, 2001.

NOTE: The UN defines "least-developed nations" to be a subset of "less-developed nations." By contrast, these charts completely separate the two categories, removing the "least-developed" nations from the "less-developed."

**Figure 1.1—Shares of the World Population by Levels of
Regional Development, 1950, 2000, and 2050**

In addition to the effect of population numbers on the demand for fixed resources, there is also a potentially negative impact of population growth on capital intensity. In principle, higher population numbers require more homes, factories, and infrastructure to house, employ, and provide for their needs. In the long run, such capital can be constructed, but periods of rapid population growth may well lead to reductions in capital per worker and lower living standards. When population growth is rapid, a large part of investment is used to supply the needs of the growing population rather than enabling an increase in the level of provision per capita.

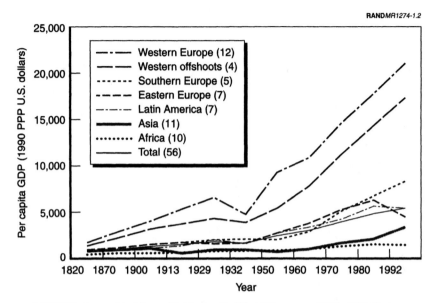

RANDMR1274-1.2

SOURCE: Angus Maddison, *Monitoring the World Economy: 1820–1992*, Paris: OECD, 1995.

NOTE: (*n*) = number of countries; PPP= purchasing power parity; Western offshoots = the United States, Canada, Australia, and New Zealand.

Figure 1.2—Economic Growth, 1820–1992 (by Major Region)

Both these theories give grounds for pessimism. However, by the early 1980s, economists were beginning to reject the pessimist view. Empirical research had weakened the pessimists' case; economic theory had begun to give increasing importance to technology and human capital accumulation rather than to the old key growth factor of physical capital; and demographic theory started to look to the intermediate and long term, where the short-term effects of population growth were likely to have at least partly smoothed out.[2] In response to these developments, organizations such as the National Academy of Sciences began to revise their earlier views, as economists' voices,

---

[2]On the importance of human capital in explaining differences in standards of living across countries, see Mankiw, Romer, and Weil (1992). On demographics, see A. C. Kelley (2001).

with their greater faith in markets' ability to respond to population growth, no longer took a backseat to those of the social and biological scientists who previously dominated population thinking (National Research Council, 1986).

THE "OPTIMISTIC" THEORY: POPULATION GROWTH CAN FUEL ECONOMIC GROWTH

Recent history has cast further doubt on the pessimists' theory. In the last 30 years—during which the world's population has doubled—per capita incomes have increased by about two-thirds. Famines have occurred, but Ehrlich's "hundreds of millions" of people have not starved. The famines that have occurred were largely caused by poverty and lack of funds within a section of the population to buy food rather than by any absolute shortage of food. (As Amartya Sen has noted, there has never been a famine in a functioning democracy, whatever its population growth rate [Sen, 1999].) Technological progress, in both agriculture and industry, has been more rapid than during any other time in human history. There have been equally dramatic social and institutional innovations: in the way people work, the standard of their education and health, and the extent to which they participate in the political process (Sen, 1999; Bloom, Craig, and Malaney, 2001). Rather than being constrained by fixed resources, the prices of many raw materials are in long-term decline, and some parts of the economy are becoming "dematerialized" as knowledge becomes an increasingly vital asset (World Bank, 1997; Task Force on Higher Education and Society, 2000).

These trends have supported the views of a group of "population optimists" who have sought to promote the idea that population growth can be an economic asset. Simon Kuznets and Julian Simon, for example, argued (separately) that as populations increase, so does the stock of human ingenuity. Larger societies—with the capacity to take advantage of economies of scale—are better positioned to develop, exploit, and disseminate the increased flow of knowledge they receive (Kuznets, 1960, 1967). Simon, in his influential book *The Ultimate Resource* (1981), showed that rapid population growth can actually lead to positive impacts on economic development (Simon, 1981). As one example, he cites the tendency of natural resource prices to decline in the long term because of technological progress induced by the growing demands of rising populations. Ester Boserup uses similar arguments to turn the Malthusian world-view around. Population growth creates pressure on resources. People are resourceful and are stimulated to innovate, especially in adversity. When rising populations swamped traditional hunter-gatherer arrangements, slash-burn-cultivate agriculture emerged. When that, too, became inadequate, intensive multi-annual cropping was developed (Boserup, 1965, 1981). More recently the Green Revolution, which has almost quadrupled world food production since 1950 using just 1 percent more land, was a direct reaction to population pressure. "Without high yield agriculture," comments Norman Borlaug, an initiator of the Green Revolution, "either millions would have starved or increases in food output would have been realized through losses of pristine land a hundred times greater than all losses to urban and suburban expansion" (Department for International Development, 1997).

The Optimists, while refuting the alarmist tendencies of the Pessimists' theory, were not dogmatic about the positive impacts of population growth. Instead, they took a broader view, suggesting that a multiplicity of external factors was responsible for the consequences of population growth. These factors could have either positive or negative economic consequences; as T. N. Srinivasan said, "Many of the alleged deleterious consequences result more from inappropriate policies and institutions than from rapid population growth" (Srinivasan, 1988). This broadening of the discussion on population growth eventually led to population *neutralism* emerging as the dominant view in the demographic debate.[3]

---

[3]A more recent position is that of Galor and Weil (1999), who propose that the Malthusian and growth regimes should not be seen as competitors but rather, respectively, the beginning and end of a historical process. The world begins in the Malthusian regime and eventually evolves from an intermediate stage they call Post-Malthusian into the current Modern Growth Regime.

THE "NEUTRALIST" THEORY: POPULATION GROWTH
HAS NO SIGNIFICANT EFFECT ON ECONOMIC GROWTH

In his pathbreaking *Inquiry into the Nature and Causes of the Wealth of Nations*, Adam Smith (1776) asked why some countries were richer than others. He found his answer in the division of labor, which allowed workers to become more productive by honing their skills at ever more specialized tasks. In recent years, economists considering the economic effects of demographic change have been more interested in Adam Smith, and in his narrative of the power of the market, than in Thomas Malthus's dire predictions about population.

Most economic analysis has examined the statistical correlation between population and economic growth and found little significant connection. Though countries with rapidly growing populations tend to have more slowly growing economies (see Figure 1.3), this negative correlation typically disappears (or even reverses direction) once other factors such as country size, openness to trade,[4] educational attainment of the population, and the quality of civil and political institutions are taken into account. Figure 1.4 shows the portion of economic growth unexplained by these other factors. It shows that this "residual" growth bears little correlation to population growth rates. In other words, when controlling for other factors, there is little cross-country evidence that population growth impedes or promotes economic growth.[5] This result seems to justify a third view: population neutralism.

The neutralist theory has been the dominant view since the mid-1980s (Bloom and Freeman, 1986). Although there are some variations within the neutralist school—with the NAS concluding in 1986 that "*on balance* ... slower population growth would be beneficial to economic development of *most* developing countries" (National Research Council, 1986; italics added), and many World Bank

---

[4]Sachs and Warner (1995) judge openness to trade on the basis of tariffs, quotas and licensing, black-market premia, and export taxes.

[5]This result refers to the average experience across countries. The economic performance of any specific country, however, will be determined by many forces.

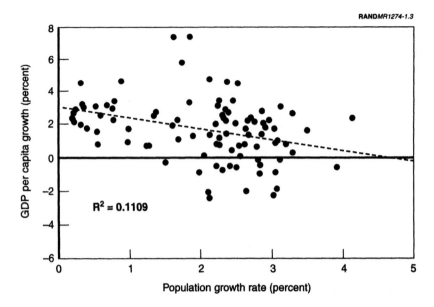

SOURCES: Authors' calculations, based on GDP data from Heston and Summers (1995) and on population growth rate data from United Nations, "World Population Prospects: The 2000 Revision," CD-ROM, 2001.

Figure 1.3—GDP per Capita Growth Against Population Growth, 1965–1990

economists suggesting that in some countries bigger populations can boost economic growth[6]—the overall tendency is to accord population issues a relatively minor place in the context of the wider policy environment.

Allen Kelley has suggested that population neutralism has in fact been the predominant school in thinking among academics about population growth for the last half-century; for example, the academic background papers to even the most pessimistic UN and NAS reports are much more moderate in tone than the reports themselves (Kelley, 2001). Kelley cites three major research areas that influenced the rise of population neutralism in the 1980s:

---

[6]See Easterly (2001), especially Chapter 5.

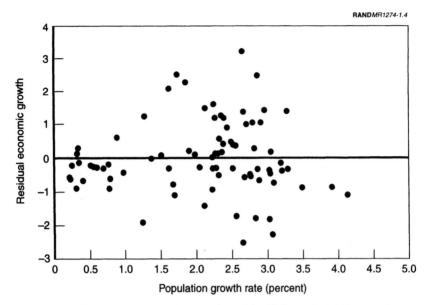

SOURCES: Authors' calculations, based on GDP data from Heston and Summers (1995) and on population growth rate data from United Nations, "World Population Prospects: The 2000 Revision," CD-ROM, 2001.

**Figure 1.4—Overall Population Growth Rate and
the Economic Growth Residual**

- **Natural Resources.** Exhaustion of natural resources was found not to be as strongly affected by population growth as the Pessimists thought. Technology, conservation, and efficient market allocation of resources all play a part in preserving natural resources, and per capita income has been shown to be a key determinant of supply and demand for these resources.

- **Saving.** The negative impact of population growth on savings (and a consequent negative effect on economic growth) was not borne out by studies.

- **Diversification of Resources.** Whereas the Pessimists had thought that population growth would lead to a diversion of resources from the formation of physical capital (which would yield quick returns) to the formation of social capital (e.g., child health and education, whose returns would take longer to be realized), multi-country studies showed that this did not in fact happen to any great extent.

According to Kelley, these studies, coupled with the impact of Julian Simon's *The Ultimate Resource* on extending demographers' view into the longer term, were crucial in bringing neutralism to the fore, and the theory has since had an enormous influence on policy-makers in developing countries and on the international development community. The Reagan administration and several donor agencies sought to limit support of population programs and simultaneously appealed to neutralist theory.[7]

THE IMPORTANCE OF AGE STRUCTURE

Proponents of population pessimism, optimism, and neutralism can all fall back on theoretical models and more or less robust data to support their positions.

All of these theories, however, tend to ignore a critical dimension of population dynamics: populations' evolving *age structure*. Economists have tended to focus on population *growth*, ignoring the changing age distribution within populations as they grow.[8] Yet these changes are arguably as important as population growth. Each age group in a population behaves differently, with distinct economic consequences: The young require intensive investment in health and

---

[7]World Bank economists had long thought that the macroeconomic case for population lending was weak (Steven W. Sinding, Professor of Clinical Public Health, Columbia University, personal communication), and excluded population issues from most policy discussions (Tom Merrick, Senior Population and Reproductive Health Adviser, World Bank, personal communication). The Reagan administration's Mexico City policy in 1984 stated that "population is neither a positive nor a negative factor" in development, but is neutral. This statement was associated with the new policy of denying federal funding to NGOs that performed or promoted abortion as a means of fertility regulation in other nations. This policy, which had been overturned by President Clinton in 1993, was reinstated by the George W. Bush administration in January 2001.

[8]The most famous exception was the seminal Coale–Hoover study, which used India and Mexico as case studies to emphasize the costs associated with a high dependency ratio in the early stage of the demographic transition. See Coale and Hoover (1958). See also Bloom and Freeman (1988).

education, prime-age adults supply labor and savings, and the aged require health care and retirement income (Figure 1.5 is a schematic representation of life cycle income and consumption). When the relative size of each of these groups in a population changes, so does the relative intensity of these economic behaviors. (Figure 1.6 illustrates the period of high population growth preceding the period during which there is a high share of working-age people.) This matters significantly to a country's income growth prospects. Policymakers with a broad view of development and the complex relation between economic and human development must factor these effects of changing age structure into decisions about their countries' future.

This challenge is especially pressing in the developing world. In those countries whose mortality and fertility rates are beginning to fall (South Central Asia and much of sub-Saharan Africa, for example), there is an opportunity for governments to capitalize on the consequent demographic transition, where the number of working-age adults grows large relative to the dependent population and

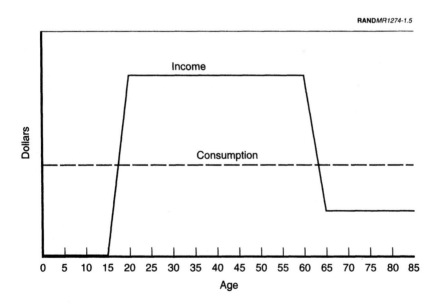

RANDMR1274-1.5

Figure 1.5—Life Cycle Income and Consumption

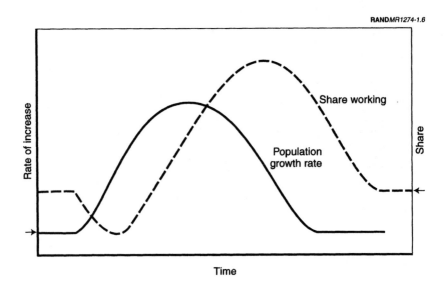

Figure 1.6—Population Growth and Age Structure

potentially acts as a major economic spur. Conversely, if the appropriate policy environment is not in place, unemployment and instability may result, and health, education, and social welfare systems may undergo unbearable strain. Those developing countries whose transition is advanced, on the other hand (Southeast Asia and Latin America), need to look to the future, adopting policies to cope with an aging population and optimize the remaining years of low dependency ratios.[9]

In Chapter Two, we assess how countries can make the most of the age structure of their populations. In Chapter Three, we examine the interplay between demographic change and economic growth within specific regions of the world. In Chapter Four, we explore how several key policy variables—health, family planning, education, and economic policies—influence a nation's ability to exploit its demographic dividend. We conclude in Chapter Five by restating the significance of population age structure—a variable that has been

---

[9]The United Nations defines "dependency ratio" as the ratio of the population aged 0–14 and 65+ to the population aged 15–64.

underappreciated in the policy debate—and clarifying how demography provides an opportunity for countries, especially for developing countries, to flourish.

Chapter Two

DEMOGRAPHIC TRANSITIONS AND THE "DEMOGRAPHIC DIVIDEND"

This chapter examines the "demographic transition" that all countries experience as social and economic development progresses, discusses the mechanisms by which its impacts are felt, and highlights the opportunity for economic growth—the "demographic dividend"—that this transition offers to developing nations.

THE DEMOGRAPHIC TRANSITION: DECLINING MORTALITY AND FERTILITY

In much of the developing world, a demographic transition is under way, accelerating with the declines in mortality that began near the end of World War II. Improvements in medicine and public health—for instance, the introduction of antibiotics such as penicillin; treatments for diseases such as tuberculosis and diarrhea; and the use of DDT, which helps control malaria—have contained or eradicated diseases that once killed millions of people (Bloom, River Path Associates, and Fang, 2000). These advances were accompanied by improved sanitation, better nutrition, and the wider practice of healthier behaviors. All this gradually led to greater life expectancies, by as much as 20 years in some countries, and naturally to population growth, especially in developing regions (see Figures 2.1 and 2.2). But despite higher life expectancies, these countries had populations that were, on average growing *younger*.[1] This is because mortality declines were not evenly distributed across the population. Infectious diseases are particularly ruthless killers of the young, so their containment had the most powerful impact on the mortality of infants and children, which fell earlier and more quickly than mortality at other ages. (Figure 2.3 shows the decline in infant mortality rates over time, and highlights the difference between more- and less-developed countries.) The larger surviving youth cohorts served to drive down the average age of populations.

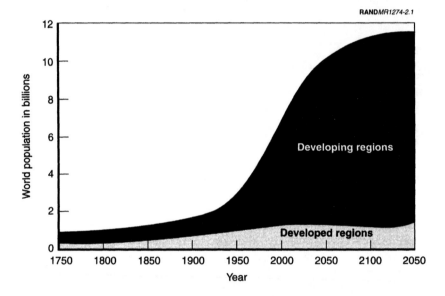

SOURCE: Population Reference Bureau, *Human Population: Fundamentals of Growth, Population Growth, and Distribution*, 2001. Available at http://www.prb.org/ Content/NavigationMenu/PRB/Educators/Human_Population/Population_Growth/ Population_Growth.htm.

Figure 2.1—World Population, 1750–2150

---

[1]From 1950 to 1960, the median age decreased in all regions and subregions of Africa, Asia, and Latin America. This time period captures the early stages of the demographic transition in most of the developing world. See United Nations (2001).

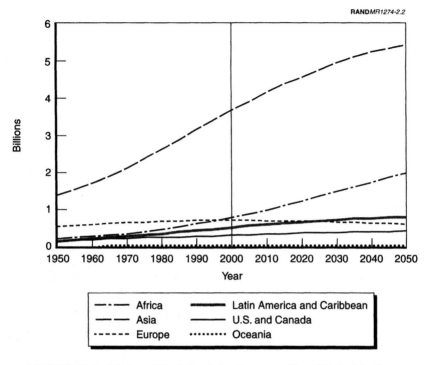

RANDMR1274-2.2

SOURCE: United Nations, "World Population Prospects: The 2000 Revision,"
CD-ROM, 2001.
NOTE: Post-2000 data are UN projections.

Figure 2.2—Population by Region, 1950–2050

The mortality decline, which began the demographic transition, has
been succeeded by equally dramatic reductions in fertility, especially
in less-developed countries (see Figure 2.4). Fertility decisions seem
to respond strongly to changes in child mortality as parents realize
that if fewer children are likely to die in childhood, they can give
birth to fewer children to attain their desired number of offspring.
This desire to rein in fertility is reflected in trends in the use of contraceptives. Worldwide, more than half of all couples now use contraception, compared with 10 percent in the 1960s (Department for
International Development, 1997). In Bangladesh, for example, the

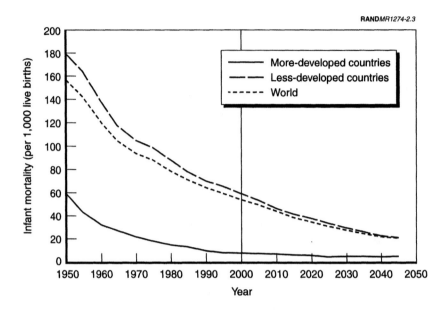

SOURCE: United Nations, "World Population Prospects: The 2000 Revision,"
CD-ROM, 2001.
NOTE: Post-2000 data are UN projections.

**Figure 2.3—Trends in the Infant Mortality Rate
at Different Levels of Development**

percentage of couples using contraception tripled, to 31 percent, in
just 14 years (1975–89) (Shahid Ullah and Chakraborty, 1993).

Other changes have reinforced the trend toward lower fertility, as it
becomes advantageous to have smaller families. If children have a
higher chance of survival and a long life expectancy, it is wise to invest intensively in them. A major form of investment is education—
an investment that becomes more tempting when economic changes
are likely to increase the potential returns on education. But this requires a long-term commitment. In a rural society, children typically
start working on the land quite early and become economically productive at a young age. Educating children limits their productivity
during childhood (they are at school rather than working). However,

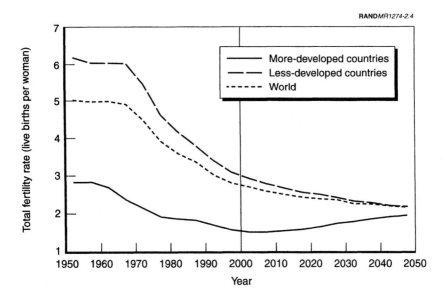

SOURCE: United Nations, "World Population Prospects: The 2000 Revision," CD-ROM, 2001.
NOTE: Post-2000 data are UN projections.

Figure 2.4—Trends in the Fertility Rate at Different Levels of Development

with increasing urbanization, children are less likely to be economically productive and the labor market will place a greater premium on skills, so education makes a greater difference to their future productivity. Thus urbanization raises the incentive of parents to educate their children while it reduces the opportunity cost of education in terms of forgone labor income. Because education is expensive, it becomes more likely that couples will choose to invest greater resources in fewer children. In addition, a greater emphasis on education will inevitably lead to more educated women. This reinforces the likelihood that families will become smaller: Women's time becomes more valuable and they are less likely to want to spend so much of their adult life bearing and raising children (Birdsall, Kelley, and Sinding, 2001, p. 13). For many reasons, then, smaller families make increasingly sound economic sense once the demographic transition gets under way.[2]

The decline in mortality and the decline in fertility jointly form the demographic transition, but they are not synchronized. The lag between the two causes population growth, as fertility only begins to decline some time after mortality has dropped (see Figure 2.5). This growth at the beginning of the demographic transition has preoccupied the prevailing views of population change and economic growth. However, the demographic transition also has a predictable impact on a country's age structure. At first, there is a cohort of children that includes many who would previously have suffered an early death. This baby-boom generation is unique: As fertility rates decline and families grow smaller, successive cohorts tend to be smaller. The result is a "bulge" in the age structure, a "demographic wave" that works its way through the population. (Figures 2.6, 2.7, and 2.8 show this moving bulge, and successive waves of it, for developing countries as a whole, East Asia, and Ireland, respectively. Figure 2.9 shows that only the beginnings of such a bulge are evident in sub-Saharan Africa.)

These figures reflect the age-structure effects of the demographic transition. First, there are many young people, who need to be fed, clothed, housed, cared for medically, and educated. Then, they become adults who are more likely to spend only part of the income they generate on their own needs. The rest is used to provide for children or is saved, most often for retirement. Finally, there is a large cohort of elderly people, who work less—or not at all—and become "dependent" again. They either live off their own savings or are supported by their families or the state.

The effects of the modern demographic transition can be felt for several generations. An initial spurt of population growth occurs between the beginning of the mortality decline and the end of the fertility decline. But when the baby-boom generation itself reaches the prime reproductive years, it creates its own echo: a succeeding baby boom. Subsequent echo effects produce further spurts. In other

---

[2]Montgomery, Aruends-Kuenning, and Mete (1999) discuss the dynamics between fertility rates and education in Asia.

RAND*MR1274-2.5*

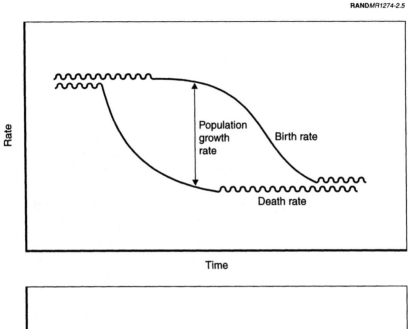

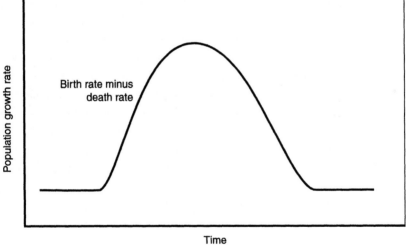

Figure 2.5—The Demographic Transition, and Population Growth Rate over the Course of the Demographic Transition

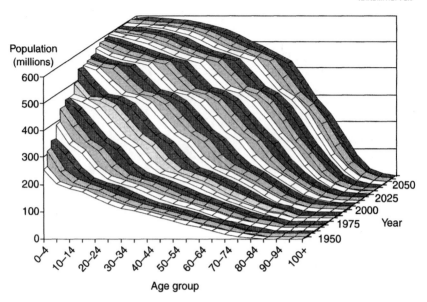

SOURCE: United Nations, "World Population Prospects: The 2000 Revision," CD-ROM, 2001.

Figure 2.6—Population by Age Group and Year, Less-Developed Regions

words, even if total fertility rates have been reduced to replacement level (2.1 children per woman), the population will continue to grow until the members of the bulge generation and successive echo generations tend to have passed through their prime reproductive years.[3] This process is called population momentum, and its effects will be felt for perhaps 50 to 100 years before the population age structure settles down. Because of the effect of population momentum alone, the population of developing countries as a whole is expected to increase by 40 percent between 1995 and 2100 (Bongaarts, 1999; Bloom, 1999).

---

[3]Assuming constant rates of age-specific fertility, the echo generations will perturb the age structure of the population in less and less pronounced fashion, as they are further removed from the initial baby boom.

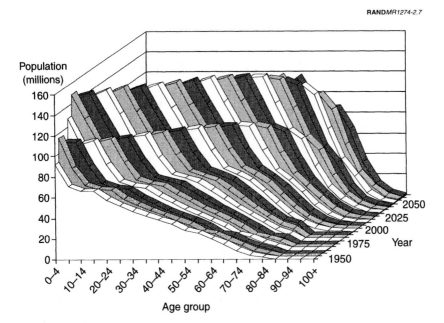

RAND*MR1274-2.7*

SOURCE: United Nations, "World Population Prospects: The 2000 Revision," CD-ROM, 2001.

Figure 2.7—Population by Age Group and Year, East Asia

While many economists have studied the effect of population growth on economic growth, far less attention has been paid to changes in the age structure brought about by the demographic transition. Combining the population growth rate and the growth rate of the *economically active* population captures the way that age structures change and delivers striking results.[4] While population growth has a large and statistically significant negative effect on per capita income

---

[4]The economically active population comprises all persons of either sex who furnish the supply of labor for the production of economic goods and services as defined by the United Nations systems of national accounts and balances during a specified time-reference period (International Labour Office, 1996).

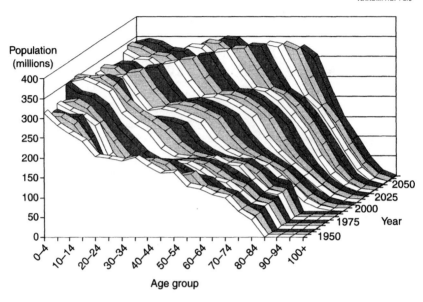

SOURCE: United Nations, "World Population Prospects: The 2000 Revision," CD-ROM, 2001.

Figure 2.8—Population by Age Group and Year, Ireland

growth, this effect is counteracted by a statistically significant positive effect from growth in the share of the population that is economically active. While the age structure remains constant, therefore, the effect of population growth is neutral, but as the proportion of workers rises or falls, so do opportunities for economic growth. The demographic dividend, for example, was essential to East Asia's extraordinary economic achievements, accounting for as much as one-third of its "economic miracle" (Bloom and Williamson, 1998; Bloom, Canning, and Malaney, 2000).

Ireland is another country in which demographic events have had a powerful impact on economic growth. Ireland had been slow to complete the demographic transition. Before 1980, Ireland's total fertility rate was very high by European standards, with more than

3.5 births per woman. One reason for this was undoubtedly the legal ban on the use of contraception. However, in 1979 contraceptives were made available with a doctor's prescription, and from 1985 on contraceptives could be sold to all those aged 18 and over. As a result, the crude birth rate in Ireland fell sharply, from 21.0 per thousand to 14.2 per thousand between 1980 and 1990. The falling birth rate led, of course, to falling youth dependency and a higher share of working-age people. It also encouraged rapid economic growth. From 1960 to 1990, the growth rate of income per capita was approximately 3.5 percent per annum. In the 1990s, this growth rate jumped to 5.8 percent, which is well in excess of any other European economy, thereby giving rise to the notion of the "Irish Tiger."

Economic growth in Ireland was also fueled by two additional factors that increased labor supply per capita. The period 1980–2000 saw a large increase in female labor force participation rates. While one would expect rapid economic growth to encourage female labor participation, it seems likely that at least some of the increase was due to the availability of contraception and the increased freedom of women to choose between working and rearing children. In addition, Ireland has historically had large levels of outward migration of young adults (around 1 percent of the population per year) due to the inability of its economy to absorb the large inflows of young workers created by its high fertility rate. The loss of these young workers of course exacerbated the problem of the high youth dependency rate. The economic growth of the 1990s created enough jobs to reverse this flow, resulting in a small net immigration of workers, mainly from Eastern Europe.

It is worth noting that Ireland, like the "miracle" economies of East Asia, had in place the right economic policies to take advantage of the demographic forces it has experienced. Two key policies were at work in Ireland. First, in the late 1950s, there was recognition that the "closed economy" model of development had failed in Ireland. This led to new polices with an emphasis on encouraging direct foreign investment in Ireland and promoting exports. Second, from the mid-1960s, free secondary education was introduced, leading to a large increase in school enrollments and subsequent expansions in higher education. The resultant high levels of education, combined with export-oriented economic policies, seem to be powerful factors in ensuring that the benefits of the demographic transition are realized.

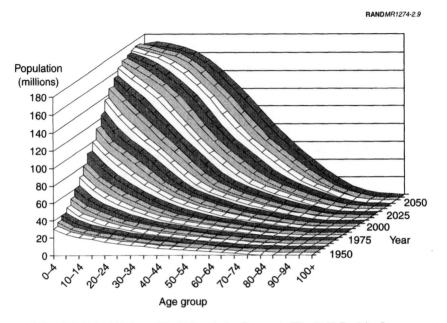

RAND*MR1274-2.9*

SOURCE: United Nations, "World Population Prospects: The 2000 Revision," CD-ROM, 2001.

Figure 2.9—Population by Age Group and Year, Sub-Saharan Africa

Demographic change in Ireland encouraged economic growth, but it did so because of key enabling aspects of the policy environment. Without the right policy environment, countries will be too slow to adapt to their changing age structure and, at best, will miss an opportunity to secure high growth. At worst, where an increase in the working-age population is not matched by increased job opportunities, they will face costly penalties, such as rising unemployment and perhaps also higher crime rates and political instability. With no policies in place to provide for rising numbers of old people, many may face destitution in their final years (Bloom and Williamson, 1998).

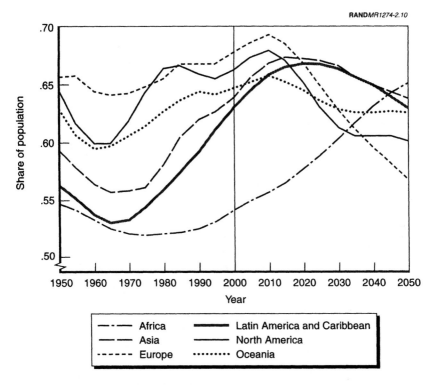

RAND*MR1274-2.10*

SOURCE: United Nations, "World Population Prospects: The 2000 Revision," CD-ROM, 2001.

Figure 2.10—Share of Working-Age Population by Region

In addition, the demographic dividend is time-limited. Many developed nations are facing the end of their demographic transition, and now must plan for their aging populations and a decline in their ratio of workers to dependents. Figure 2.10 shows how the share of the population that is of working age has varied and is expected to vary over time in different regions of the world. Figure 2.11 highlights the same phenomena for East Asia, sub-Saharan Africa, and Ireland. In all regions except Africa, the share of the population that is of working age will begin to decrease in the next 10–20 years.

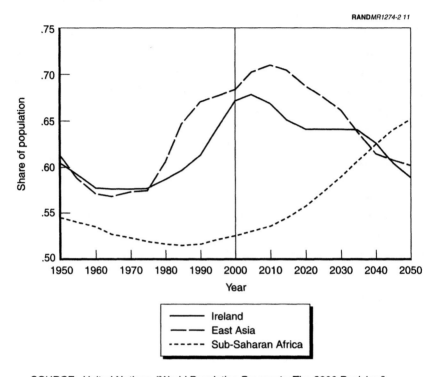

SOURCE: United Nations, "World Population Prospects: The 2000 Revision,"
CD-ROM, 2001.
NOTE: Post-2000 data are UN projections.

Figure 2.11—Share of Population of Working Age, Specific Areas

Additionally, some are experiencing shrinking populations. Low fertility rates over an extended period of time, where replacement level is not reached, eventually lead to population decline. Italy's population, currently at 57 million, is projected to decline to 43 million by 2050. Japan's population is expected to decrease from 127 million to 109 million by 2050 (United Nations, 2001). The available labor force will decrease, and the elderly will increasingly make up a larger proportion of the population, bringing with it further social and economic challenges (Bloom, Nandakumar, and Bhawalkar, 2001). Through the lens of demography at least, the next 50 years presents the developed world with significant challenges, at the same time as it offers the developing world a number of appealing opportunities.[5]

The Demographic "Dividend"

The demographic dividend is delivered through a number of mechanisms. The most important are labor supply, savings, and human capital.

Labor Supply. The demographic transition affects labor supply in two ways. First, there is an essentially mechanical effect, based on the regular and inevitable aging of the baby-boom generation (Bloom, Canning, and Sevilla, 2000). When this generation is between 15 and 64, it is more likely to be working, thus lowering the ratio of dependents to nondependents. (Figure 2.12 shows labor force participation rates by age group in various regions of the world.) During the peak working years of 20 to 54, this effect is especially strong. The number of people who would like to work (labor supply) therefore gets bigger and, provided the labor market can absorb the larger numbers of workers, per capita production increases.

Second, women are more likely to enter the workforce as family size declines. This effect is magnified by the fact that, with adult women

---

[5]See Teitelbaum and Winter (1985). Also, it is worth noting that a declining population, particularly in a country such as Japan, can carry with it the benefit of lessened pressure on natural resources. If the degradation of natural resource capital were accounted for properly, the trajectory of net national income would, other things equal, rise more quickly (or decline more slowly) as compared with that of a stationary or growing population. In addition, population decline does not necessarily translate into a comparable decline in the size of the labor force. This is due to the potential for (a) increased labor force participation among women, (b) increased retirement age, and (c) increases in net immigration, which tends to be selective of working-age individuals. Differences between the male and female labor force participation rate in Italy (23 percentage points) and Japan (21 percentage points) are higher than for most high-income countries (e.g., the differences for France and the United Kingdom are 12 percentage points and 14 percentage points, respectively) (see World Bank [2001] World Development Indicators; data for 1999). In addition, retirement ages have been relatively stagnant in comparison with life expectancy. Between 1965 and 2000, Italy's life expectancy increased from 71 to 79, and Japan's from 71 to 81. By comparison, retirement age in Italy is 62 for both men and women (up from 61 for men and 56 for women during that period) and 65 in Japan. An upward adjustment of the retirement age could mitigate the labor force effects of population aging. Finally, for more on immigration, see McCarthy (2001).

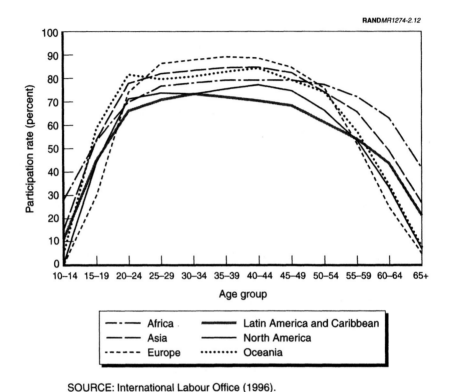

SOURCE: International Labour Office (1996).

**Figure 2.12—Labor Force Participation by Age Group,
in Various Regions of the World, 1990**

themselves more likely to have been brought up in small families, they are more likely to be educated. This increases their productivity in the labor market, leading toward a stronger workforce and smaller families.

Savings. The demographic transition also encourages the growth of savings, thus improving a country's prospects for investment and growth. Again, there is an accounting effect as well as a behavioral effect at work. The young and the old consume more than they produce, whereas working-age people tend to have a higher level of economic output and also a higher level of savings (Higgins, 1998; Higgins and Williamson, 1997; Kelley and Schmidt,, 1996; Lee, Mason, and Miller, 2000; Leff, 1969; Mason, 1988; Webb and Zia, 1990). Further, people tend to save more between the ages of 40 and 65, when they are less likely to be investing in their children and the need to prepare for their retirement is becoming more pressing.[6] So when large numbers of baby boomers start hitting their 40s, national savings will tend to rise.[7] Incentives to make certain choices can reinforce this tendency to save among the new young baby boomers. Improved health, and longevity, make saving easier and more attractive (Meltzer, 1992). A healthy population must plan far in advance if it is to maintain its standard of living through decades of retirement (Lee, Mason, and Miller, 2000). Pensions are made even more important by smaller families and the mobility that urbanization brings. An extended family often takes care of its own elderly relatives. A nuclear family, with both parents working, is far less likely to do so, although the two-earner family's increased assets make it better able to provide care financially, if not physically. Additionally, private household savings can provide the capital accumulation needed to finance growth, as seen in East Asia (Krugman, 1994; Young, 1994, 1995; Asian Development Bank, 1997, pp. 141–197; Higgins, 1998; Kelley and Schmidt, 1995, 1996). Further work is needed, however, to take account of the institutional features of pension systems when assessing the importance of the demographic transition to the determination of national savings.

Human Capital. Finally, the demographic transition has significant effects on investments in human capital, effects which are the least tangible, but may be the most significant and far-reaching. The demographic transition begins with changes in mortality that result in a population that lives longer and stays healthier. A longer life expectancy causes fundamental changes in the way that people live. Attitudes about education, family, retirement, the role of women, and work all tend to shift. A society, especially if it is taking full advantage of the demographic dividend, is certain to experience deep-

---

[6]These conclusions are based on data are from household surveys (Paxson, 1996; Deaton and Paxson, 1997). Coale and Hoover (1958) suggest that the dip in savings rate for people in their early 30s is related to the consumption needs of people with young families.

[7]Studies examining the relationship between age structure and savings include Leff (1969); Mason (1981, 1987); Webb and Zia (1990); Kelley and Schmidt (1996); Higgins and Williamson (1997); and Bloom, Canning, and Graham (2002).

rooted changes in its culture, as its people become more valuable assets. Take education, for example: The positive correlation between education and earnings is well-known. In Latin America, for example, a worker with six years of education earns an average of 50 percent more than one who has no formal education. The premium increases to 120 percent for those with 12 years of education (i.e., those finishing secondary school), and exceeds 200 percent for those with 17 years of education (i.e., those completing tertiary education) (Inter-American Development Bank, 1999). As life expectancy increases, parents are likely to choose to educate their children to more advanced levels. Healthier children, in turn, tend to experience greater cognitive development per year of schooling than their less healthy counterparts (Jamison et al., 1996). The parents also know that there is a good chance that each child will benefit from schooling investments over a long working life and, with fewer children, can devote more time and money to each child. The result of this educational investment is that the labor force as a whole becomes more productive, promoting higher wages and a better standard of living. Women and men therefore tend to enter the workforce later, partly because they are being educated for longer, but they are likely to be more productive once they start working (International Labour Office, 1996; Bloom, Canning, and Sevilla, 2001).

All these mechanisms are heavily dependent on the policy environment. A growing number of adults will only be productive if there is sufficient flexibility in the labor market to allow its expansion, and if there are macroeconomic policies that permit and encourage investment. Similarly, people will only save if they have access to adequate saving mechanisms and have confidence in domestic financial markets. Finally, the demographic transition creates conditions where people will tend to invest in their own and their children's health and education, offering great economic benefits, especially in the modern world's increasingly sophisticated economies. But governments invariably play a vital role in creating an environment where high-quality health and education provision is possible—necessary steps to make the most of their country's demographic opportunities.

Chapter Three

CASE STUDIES OF POPULATION CHANGE AND ECONOMIC GROWTH

This chapter examines the interplay between population change and economic growth within specific regions of the world: East Asia; Japan; North America, Western Europe, Australia, and New Zealand; South Central and Southeast Asia; Latin America; the Middle East and North Africa; sub-Saharan Africa; and Eastern Europe and the former Soviet Union. The East Asian nations have experienced the most success in exploiting the "demographic dividend" made available by reduced fertility. Latin America has undergone a less dramatic transition and has had far less success in creating conditions for economic growth. The Middle East and North Africa are still in much earlier stages of the demographic transition, and indeed many parts of sub-Saharan Africa have seen virtually no decreases in traditionally high fertility rates. Japan, a developed country with an aging population, illustrates the "back end" of the demographic transition: It is facing the issues posed by a declining workforce and an increasing ratio of elderly dependents. Eastern Europe and the former Soviet Union also have aging populations and very low birth rates that will present challenges.

EAST ASIA

The East Asian "economic miracle" offers some of recent history's most compelling evidence of the "demographic dividend."[1] The East Asian demographic transition occurred with relative rapidity, over a 50–75-year period—the fastest demographic transition to date.[2] Modern transitions are faster because countries gain the benefit of knowledge, experience, or technology developed by others.[3]

Throughout the world, dramatic improvements in public health emerged from the late 1940s onward, largely through improved sanitation, safer water, and the development of broad-spectrum antibiotics and antimicrobials (for example, penicillin, sulfa drugs, streptomycin, bacitracin, chloroquine, and tetracycline, discovered and introduced between 1920 and 1940, and the use of DDT from 1943). From the 1950s onward, there were significant and sustained declines in infant and child mortality. The infant mortality rate (the proportion of babies who die before their first birthday) in East Asia dropped from 181 per 1,000 in 1950 to 34 per 1,000 in 2000 (United Nations, 2001). In time, the effect of the decrease in mortality carried through to a fall in fertility rates. This was assisted by family planning programs, which made contraceptives both easier to obtain and more socially acceptable. In the 1950s, East Asia's developing countries used voluntary programs of incentives to encourage families to have fewer children, and the transition from high to replacement-level fertility took less than 30 years (Mason, 2001). In 1950, the typical East Asian woman had 6 children; today she has 2. In the lag between the decrease in infant mortality and the decline in fertility, a baby-boom generation was created.[4]

---

[1]See Mason (2001) for a detailed and compelling set of analyses on similar topics that reach similar conclusions. Among other topics, Mason addresses the possibility of reverse causality, i.e., from economic growth to demographic change.

[2]In Western Europe, for example, the process began in the mid-18th century and was to last nearly 150 years. In Sweden, the transition took even longer, occupying the better part of 300 years; see also Bloom, Nandakumar, and Bhawalkar (2001).

[3]In Ireland, for example, since modern contraception was legalized—first among married couples, and then generally—there has been a steep decline in fertility since the early 1980s.

[4]The working-age population rose from around 57 percent of East Asia's total population in 1965 to around 68 percent in 2000.

The East Asian demographic transition was one of the critical factors in the region's spectacular economic growth (Bloom and Williamson, 1998; Bloom, Canning, and Malaney, 2000). Between 1965 and 1990, per capita income rose annually by more than 6 percent. One explanation for this phenomenal growth is that in the late 1960s, when the baby-boom generation started work, their entry into the workforce changed the ratio of workers to dependents in the population. With the benefits of a good education and a liberalized trade environment, this generation was absorbed into the job market and into gainful employment, thereby increasing the region's capacity for economic production. The region's working-age population grew nearly four times faster (an average of 2.4 percent a year) than its dependent population between 1965 and 1990. A virtuous spiral was thus created, whereby population change increased income growth, and income growth pushed down population growth—and therefore the number of dependents—by reducing fertility.[5] East Asia's high savings rates were also affected by the demographic transition, as the baby-boom generation entered the workforce and parents had fewer children to take care of, although the extent of the effect is disputed in the literature.[6] Results from Bloom and Sachs (1998), Bloom and Williamson (1998), and Bloom, Canning, and Malaney (2000) suggest that the demographic dividend accounts for between one-fourth and two-fifths of East Asia's "economic miracle." Growth accounting exercises presented by Mason (2001) further confirms the results of the regression analyses in these works.

Yet as its baby-boom cohort ages, East Asia must prepare for an aging population. Not only did infant mortality decrease, but mortality at other ages fell as well and, as a result, life expectancy has risen from around 43 years in 1950 to 72 years today. Population growth has slowed dramatically—from a peak of 2.4 percent a year in the late 1960s, it is now 0.66 percent a year, and predicted to be only 0.2 percent by 2025. When the baby boom retires, the ratio of dependents to workers will change again, and bring added challenges to policy-

---

[5]For discussion of how the spheres of globalization, liberalization, and sustainable human development can be managed to help capture the demographic dividend, see Bloom, Mahal, King, et al. (2001).

[6]See Mason (2001) for a discussion of the literature on savings rates and the demographic transition.

makers and the economy (see detailed discussion of Japan below). Pensions and health care for the elderly will come under strain, and economic growth is likely to slow down as the labor force declines.

An aging population is, fundamentally, a mark of development success. However, the aged face a range of potential problems, including poverty (Japan has elderly poverty rates above 18 percent; see Gruber and Wise, 2001). Additionally, the speed of change in the modern world—including profound changes in family and social patterns—means that policymakers worldwide will be hard-pressed to ensure that the challenge of an aging society does not become a crisis.[7] They will also need to address the fact that a significant proportion of the elderly are women, who often suffer a double disempowerment based on age and gender.

East Asia, with its mix of advanced and developing economies, can expect a variable set of challenges to emerge in the next decade or so. The challenge is already present in some of the richest countries in the region, like Korea and Hong Kong. In the medium term, over the next decade or so, the problem of aging populations will also become more pressing in less wealthy countries such as China (see Randel, German, and Ewing, 1999).

JAPAN

Japan is perhaps the world's most rapidly aging country, with life expectancy the highest in the world. A Japanese person born today can expect to live until 81. Whereas in 1920 the median age of the population in Japan was only 27 years, today it stands at over 40 years. Fertility rates are low in Japan—at 1.3 children per woman. The consequences of Japan's rapidly aging population are already being felt, as policymakers strive to prepare for the challenge of an increasingly elderly population. Today, around four people of working age support each pensioner, but in 2025 falling birth rates are expected to halve that figure. In 1950, the ratio was 12 workers for each pensioner (United Nations, 2001).

---

[7]With more women working and a decrease in co-residence of elderly parents with their adult children, the Japanese tradition of family members looking after their elderly is waning. See Bloom, Nandakumar, and Bhawalkar (2001).

Japan is approaching the end of its demographic transition, having enjoyed the economic successes of its demographic dividend, combined with strong policies. After World War II, Japan was in economic crisis. The war had destroyed nearly half of the nation's industrial plants and infrastructure. However, with a series of policies concentrating on building modern factories, and a well-educated and highly literate workforce, Japan was able to push its economy to the forefront of technology and modernity, establishing itself as one of the world's most powerful economies.

Government/industry cooperation, a well-educated and motivated workforce, a focus on technology, and a comparatively small defense allocation (1 percent of its gross domestic product [GDP]) contributed to Japan's economic success.

But now 17 percent of Japan's population is 65 years old or over (see Figure 3.1). In 2050, 36 percent of the population will be aged 65+, with 15 percent aged 80+; the dependency ratio will rise from 0.47 to 0.96 (United Nations, 2001). Their care needs (medical, social, and financial) represent a significant challenge. Forty percent of the 65+ population in Japan live either alone or as a couple. With the breakdown of extended families, the elderly cannot depend on their families to provide for them, and the state must prepare to step into the gap.

Pensions are a particular challenge, given that many countries finance pension payments from current taxation. With a smaller, young workforce supporting a pay-as-you-go pension system, spending on pensions could push Japan's budget deficit up to 20 percent of its GDP by 2030. Pension contributions will have to increase to 35 percent of salaries to maintain the current level of payouts.

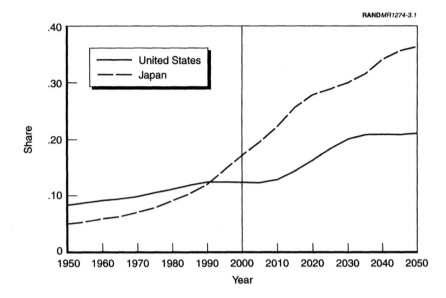

SOURCE: United Nations, "World Population Prospects: The 2000 Revision," CD-ROM, 2001.
NOTE: Post-2000 data are UN projections.

Figure 3.1—Population Share Aged 65+

Finally, with the drop in fertility rates and with many people retiring, the number of people working will become smaller, further challenging Japan's economy and slowing growth.[8] But Japan will not be alone in facing such challenges in the coming decades. Several of the available reforms proposed by, among others, the Organization for Economic Cooperation and Development,[9] including labor and product reforms and fiscal consolidation, represent good governance strategies irrespective of the aging issue. Nevertheless, the growing proportion of the elderly will no doubt present significant challenges to policymakers.

---

[8]It is estimated that Japan's labor force will fall by 13 percent between now and 2050, and that income growth will slow to 0.25 percent per year by 2040 (Turner et al., 1998).

[9]For an accessible overview see, for example, Vanston (1998).

NORTH AMERICA, WESTERN EUROPE, AUSTRALIA, AND NEW ZEALAND

The developed world has reached an advanced stage of the demographic transition. Fertility rates are below replacement level in many countries in Europe, and populations are growing at a slow pace. North America continues to grow largely because of its high rates of net in-migration and large population of childbearing age, while Western Europe's population has plateaued and will begin a slight decline in a few decades. From 2001 to 2025, the population of Europe as a whole is expected to decline by 6 percent, and that of Japan by 3 percent; North America's is expected to grow by 21 percent. Sub-Saharan Africa, on the other hand, is projected to grow by 74 percent (United Nations, 2001).

The demographic transition in the developed world began in the 19th century. Over a 100-year period (from 1861 to 1961), infant mortality in England and Wales declined from 154 deaths per 1,000 live births to 21 per 1,000. Life expectancy at birth (again, in England and Wales) also rose over that same period, with male life expectancy rising from 40 to 68. Fertility also fell, in most countries by about 50 percent between 1870 and 1940 (Teitelbaum and Winter, 1985). During the late 19th and early 20th centuries, the working-age population began to grow more quickly than the young dependent population, potentially contributing to the acceleration of economic development that occurred in the West in this period (Malmberg and Lindh, 2000). After World War II, however, increased optimism about the future saw fertility rates in the West shoot up. From a low of 2.2 children per woman in the 1930s, U.S. fertility rates rose to a high of 3.8 in 1957. The pattern in the United Kingdom, Australia, Canada, and New Zealand was similarly dramatic (Teitelbaum and Winter, 1985). Fertility rates only began to fall again in 1960, declining sharply and reaching replacement levels in the mid-1970s. Other Western European countries also experienced fertility increases after World War II, although on a smaller scale. The famous baby-boom generation was thus created. Some research finds that these post–World War II demographic changes had a significant effect on economic growth. As noted earlier, population growth among middle-aged adults can promote income growth, and population growth among the elderly tends to slow growth. Population growth among young adults, on the other hand, seems to have no effect (Lindh and Malmberg, 1999; Malmberg, 1994).

Caplow, Hicks, and Wattenberg (2001) note that fertility in the wealthy industrial countries has continued to fall, and is likely to remain below the replacement level of 2.1 births per woman well into the 21st century. The baby-boom generation is now approaching retirement age, and the continued decline in fertility rates has meant that the West now faces the problem of an aging society, where an increased cohort of elderly relies on a reduced working-age population. The UN Population Division has forecast that the percentage of people aged 60 or over in the developed regions will rise from 19 percent in 2000 to 33 percent by 2050 (United Nations, 2001). Furthermore, the dependency balance has shifted. In 1950, children made up 27 percent of the population in these regions, and people aged 60+ made up 12 percent. By 2050, however, this situation will be reversed, with the proportion of older people rising to 33 percent and that of children falling to 16 percent.

Population aging is most advanced in Europe and Japan. The median age of Europeans is expected to rise from 38 in 2000 to 49 in 2050, and the median age in Japan is already 41 (United Nations, 2001). So, whereas South Central Asia and sub-Saharan Africa's policymakers should be looking at ways to capture a future demographic dividend, the governments of the developed world, whose dividend is about to expire, are likely to find coping with an aging population high on their list of priorities. Aging populations will put pressure on social security systems, health services, and pensions, as the smaller working-age group contributes fewer taxes and the economy, potentially, shrinks.

The United States' welcoming of immigrants, which will ensure that the working-age population continues to grow, is in marked contrast to Japan's policy, where immigrants make up just 1.2 percent of the population. Notwithstanding the fact that Western Europe is more open than Japan, its population is still likely to shrink slightly and age over the next 50 years.

In many wealthy industrial countries, public-sector reform will focus on health care, pensions, and social security. Private health care and pensions are likely to become more important, along with public–

private partnerships in health care provision (Fuchs, 1999; Bloom, Craig, and Mitchell, 2000; Reich, 2000). Raising the retirement age and encouraging people to work at older ages via tax breaks and life-long training have also been suggested (Wattenberg, 1987; Bloom, Nandakumar, and Bhawalkar, 2002).

Some have even predicted great difficulties for the West as a result of the aging boom (Peterson, 2000), but changing habits—whereby people turn to private health care and pensions, retire later, and do more work for longer—are likely to soften the blow.[10] Changing immigration patterns may also play a part in averting economic difficulties.[11] The private sector is likely to have a vital role to play both in provision of public services and attracting immigration. Engaging private enterprise will require a change in attitudes, particularly in those Western European countries used to overbearing public-sector bureaucracies, so change is likely to be slow. Policymakers will have to focus on facilitating these changes, and prompt action now will ease the pain later.

SOUTH CENTRAL AND SOUTHEAST ASIA[12]

South and Southeast Asia have lagged behind East Asia in the demographic transition. However, Southeast Asia has recently begun to benefit from the demographic dividend, and South Central Asia is likely to follow (Asian Development Bank, 1997, p. 142).

---

[10]On the other hand, Weil (1999) argues that trying to forestall this process by encouraging fertility may entail its own large transitory costs.

[11]See Section 2.3 of Weil (1997) on the effects that immigration can have on slowing growth in the dependency ratio.

[12]It is often difficult to compare results across studies because the geographical definitions of different regions vary from one source to another. For example, many of the demographic statistics cited here are based on UN data and regional groupings, whereas some of the economic analysis is based on a somewhat different set of regional groupings used by the Asian Development Bank. The demographic data presented here reflect the following UN definitions: South Central Asia consists of Afghanistan, Bangladesh, Bhutan, India, Iran, Kazakhstan, Kyrgyzstan, Maldives, Nepal, Pakistan, Sri Lanka, Tajikistan, Turkmenistan, and Uzbekistan. Southeast Asia consists of Brunei Darussalam, Cambodia, East Timor, Indonesia, Laos, Malaysia, Myanmar, Philippines, Singapore, Thailand, and Vietnam.

Until 1950, population growth rates across Asia as a whole had remained relatively stable at less than 1 percent per year for at least the previous 70 years. However, from 1950 to 1990, rates in South Central and Southeast Asia shot up, averaging well over 2 percent per year. These rates were lower than in Africa, but similar to those in Latin America and well above those in East Asia, North America, and Europe. This growth can firstly be attributed to falling mortality rates. The introduction of drugs to treat diseases such as tuberculosis, scarlet fever, and pneumonia, coupled with the use of DDT to combat malaria, saw infant mortality rates in particular decline dramatically. As in East Asia, fertility declines followed the fall in mortality. Health improvements have meant that families have needed fewer children in order to ensure achieving their desired family sizes. Family planning programs have also had an impact (Asian Development Bank, 1997). The fall in Southeast Asia's fertility rate has been nearly as dramatic as that of East Asia, while South Central Asia's average number of births per woman has been nearly halved since 1960. Southeast Asia's rate is expected to come close to East Asia's rate by 2020. This will eventually lead to a decline in population growth rates to around 1 percent per year by approximately 2020 (Asian Development Bank, 1997, p. 150; United Nations, 2001).

In addition to the size of the region's population, its age structure has also changed. As shown in Table 3.1, although South Central and Southeast Asia's economically active populations grew in comparison with their economically dependent populations from 1965 to 1990, the difference was much less marked than that in East Asia. (Table 3.1 also gives the analogous figures for all regions of the world through 2015.) As a consequence, the demographic dividend has so far been less pronounced in these regions. While East Asia's working-age population made up 67 percent of the region's total population in 1990, Southeast and South Central Asia's was less than 60 percent. Moreover, the percentage in East Asia rose sharply in the 15 years after 1975 (from 57 percent to 67 percent), while in the rest of Asia it rose more slowly (from 56 percent to 58 percent in South Central Asia; from 54 percent to 59 percent in Southeast Asia; and from 54 to 57 percent in Southwest Asia). By 2025, Southeast Asia (at 68 percent) will match, and South Central Asia (at 67 percent) will nearly match, the figure for East Asia (68 percent). Consistent with this, dependency ratios have fallen more slowly in Southeast and South Central

Asia, with the latter's youth dependency ratios (the percentage of those under 15 years old relative to the working-age population) experiencing only modest declines. Between 1975 and 1990, the youth dependency ratio fell from 0.77 to 0.62 in Southeast Asia and from 0.73 to 0.65 in South Central Asia; the comparable figures for East Asia are 0.66 and 0.40.

While Southeast Asia has already gained considerable economic benefit from its demographic change (which accounts for about 1 percentage point of per capita annual income growth [Bloom and Williamson, 1998; Bloom, Canning, and Malaney, 2000]) and is likely to see this benefit reduced over the next 25 years as the population ages, South Central Asia's transition is still continuing, suggesting growing potential for economic growth. More specifically, the current demographic dividend of approximately 0.7 percentage points of per capita annual income growth could well double as the boom reaches its peak (Asian Development Bank, 1997, pp. 158–159).

To fully capitalize on the demographic dividend, however, South Central Asia would do well to follow the policy initiatives employed so successfully by East Asia. Fertility in the region is still high—at around 3.2 births per woman in 2000 (the rates in Southeast Asia and East Asia are 2.5 and 1.8, respectively [United Nations, 2001]). Family planning programs will help to push fertility rates down, and will have the corollary effect of limiting the spread of HIV/AIDS. As the Asian Development Bank (1997) and many others have shown, there is a large unmet demand for contraception across South and Southeast Asia, and eliminating all unwanted births would go a long way toward reducing fertility to replacement levels.

Education and training are other key areas that determine the success of a country's efforts to capture a demographic dividend. Although primary and secondary enrollment levels in Asia have risen dramatically in recent decades, the demand for quality tertiary education from employers and secondary school graduates and their families is as yet largely unmet. The emerging global economy places increasing emphasis on higher education. Many countries in the region may not be able to take full advantage of their favorable demographic indicators because of relatively low rates of tertiary enrollment. New approaches to funding and a new focus on high-value

Table 3.1

Annual Growth Rates of Total Population, Working-Age Population, and Non–Working-Age Population for Asia and Its Subregions (percent)

	1965–1990			1990–2015			2015–2040		
	Total	WA	NWA	Total	WA	NWA	Total	WA	NWA
WORLD	1.84	2.14	1.39	1.27	1.54	0.81	0.83	0.72	1.03
More-developed regions	0.69	0.90	0.29	0.22	0.24	0.19	-0.04	-0.53	0.82
Less-developed regions	2.23	2.63	1.70	1.52	1.87	0.94	0.98	0.94	1.07
Least-developed countries	2.52	2.50	2.55	2.54	2.78	2.26	2.05	2.47	1.44
Less-developed regions excluding China	2.39	2.63	2.07	1.78	2.20	1.14	1.19	1.30	1.00
Less-developed regions excluding the least-developed countries	2.19	2.65	1.57	1.36	1.75	0.67	0.75	0.63	0.97
Sub-Saharan Africa	2.82	2.74	2.91	2.51	2.73	2.26	1.99	2.55	1.20
AFRICA	2.77	2.77	2.77	2.36	2.67	1.99	1.84	2.28	1.18
Eastern Africa	2.92	2.86	2.98	2.50	2.71	2.26	2.05	2.61	1.30
Middle Africa	2.78	2.48	3.11	3.05	3.06	3.04	2.62	3.27	1.84
Northern Africa	2.57	2.87	2.22	1.76	2.46	0.65	1.02	1.09	0.88
Southern Africa	2.48	2.75	2.14	0.90	1.25	0.35	0.17	0.31	-0.08
Western Africa	2.83	2.70	2.98	2.66	2.97	2.30	1.92	2.57	0.97
ASIA	2.06	2.51	1.44	1.30	1.64	0.69	0.72	0.57	1.02
Eastern Asia	1.75	2.43	0.66	0.74	0.94	0.32	0.18	-0.36	1.24
South Central Asia	2.28	2.49	2.02	1.69	2.17	0.94	1.00	1.11	0.77
Southeast Asia	2.26	2.66	1.74	1.43	2.00	0.43	0.80	0.68	1.04
Western Asia	2.76	3.06	2.39	2.17	2.51	1.65	1.58	1.68	1.42

Table 3.1—continued

	1965–1990			1990–2015			2015–2040		
	Total	WA	NWA	Total	WA	NWA	Total	WA	NWA
EUROPE	0.52	0.69	0.20	-0.10	-0.00	-0.30	-0.39	-0.93	0.59
Eastern Europe	0.61	0.76	0.33	-0.40	-0.09	-1.07	-0.63	-1.10	0.36
Northern Europe	0.34	0.38	0.27	0.16	0.22	0.06	-0.05	-0.57	0.80
Southern Europe	0.60	0.79	0.22	-0.02	-0.06	0.07	-0.48	-1.13	0.60
Western Europe	0.38	0.64	-0.10	0.19	0.08	0.41	-0.16	-0.73	0.75
LATIN AMERICA AND THE CARIBBEAN	2.28	2.74	1.71	1.44	1.91	0.65	0.81	0.71	1.00
Caribbean	1.62	2.06	1.02	1.00	1.31	0.47	0.49	0.34	0.76
Central America	2.67	3.19	2.08	1.67	2.27	0.72	0.89	0.87	0.92
South America	2.23	2.67	1.64	1.41	1.85	0.64	0.81	0.68	1.05
NORTHERN AMERICA	1.01	1.40	0.37	0.93	0.99	0.79	0.65	0.24	1.37
OCEANIA	1.66	1.96	1.17	1.30	1.35	1.20	0.84	0.66	1.14
Australia/New Zealand	1.48	1.82	0.88	1.01	1.02	1.01	0.55	0.16	1.23
Melanesia	2.38	2.57	2.15	2.21	2.57	1.69	1.54	1.87	0.96
Micronesia	2.57	2.98	2.05	2.18	2.21	2.14	1.37	1.79	0.66
Polynesia	1.69	2.36	0.90	1.18	1.55	0.60	0.90	1.02	0.68

SOURCE: United Nations, "World Population Prospects: The 2000 Revision," CD-ROM, 2001.

NOTE: WA = working-age population; NWA = non-working-age population.

areas such as technology and tourism will be required if the region is to catch up with the likes of North America.[13] India, with its burgeoning information technology sector, has already seen, via job creation, remittances, and foreign direct investment (FDI), the benefits of investment in quality higher education and a focus on core new economy subjects: science and technology (Bloom and Rosovsky, 2001).

The new economy will also require a focus on lifelong training. As a country's economy moves toward producing products and services with more value added, workers will need to be retrained to cope with the demands of a flexible labor market. This should be combined with labor market flexibility. If the South Central Asian labor market cannot cope with the huge influx of workers produced by the demographic shift, a potential virtuous spiral (with a bigger labor force contributing to increased productivity and higher savings rates) could be reversed, with rising unemployment levels leading to crime, poverty, and civil disorder.

As in East Asia and the West, policy in South Central and Southeast Asia will also need to look to the long term, when the boom generation retires. Health care systems and pensions will come under pressure, and the private sector may be usefully harnessed to help drive reform efforts.

The importance of policy to the success of attempts to capture the demographic dividend was demonstrated in East Asia. Southeast Asia, whose transition is fairly well advanced, and South Central Asia, whose potential boom is yet to come, cannot assume that demography alone will guarantee economic growth. Many governments in these regions have made a good start in certain key areas—Bangladesh has had great success with family planning programs, for example; India with basic and secondary education and the technology sector; Thailand with health efforts that have limited the spread of AIDS; and many of the countries of Southeast Asia in liberalizing labor markets and attracting foreign investment. However, there is more work to be done, and, with the demographic shift advancing,

---

[13]For a fuller discussion of the importance of higher education and approaches to reforming it, see Task Force on Higher Education and Society (2000).

the quicker it is done the better. Fertility levels are still high, tertiary education is weak, and exports are underdeveloped. The potential is there for the rest of Asia to do as well as East Asia. The region's success will depend on its policymakers.

LATIN AMERICA

Latin America's population growth is following a pattern similar to East Asia's. In 1965, life expectancy in Latin America and East Asia was in the upper 50s. Following similar improvements in public health, Latin America's life expectancy now stands at 70 years, slightly behind East Asia's 72. There have also been significant reductions in infant mortality in Latin America, which decreased from 91 deaths per 1,000 live births in 1965 to 32 in 2000 (a figure very similar to East Asia's 34). The fertility rate has also fallen—from around 5 children per woman in 1975 to the present 2.5. In some countries in the region, such as Brazil, Chile, and Uruguay, the fertility rate is just above replacement level. Barbados, Cuba, and Trinidad and Tobago are far below this level. Other countries, however, have much higher rates. In Bolivia, Guatemala, Haiti, Nicaragua, and Paraguay, women are having approximately 4 children (United Nations, 2001). It may be significant that income disparities in the region are also the widest for any region in the world (although sub-Saharan Africa runs a close second).

Although Latin American demographic changes have been favorable for growth since 1970, economic growth has yet to follow the East Asian example. So while East Asia shows a GDP per capita annual growth rate between 1975 and 1995 of 6.8 percent, the growth rate for Latin America over the same period is one-eighth of that, at 0.7 percent. Although there has been much debate surrounding Latin America's failure to thrive, there appears to be a growing consensus that the heart of the matter concerns policy (Inter-American Development Bank, 2000).

The region also experienced considerable changes in economic policies, with a growing adoption of the Washington Consensus in the late 1980s and 1990s.[14] Between 1965 and 1990, Latin America was largely closed off from the world economy. By 1980, only 12 percent of the region counted as being "open" (as defined in Sachs and Warner, 1995). Cross-country regression analysis suggests that a country with a working-age population growing 3 percent per year, and 1.5 percent faster than its overall population, will see its growth boosted by 0.5 percent a year if its economy is closed, but by 1.5 percent a year if its economy is open (Bloom, Canning, Evans, et al., 1999; Inter-American Development Bank, 2000; Bloom and Canning, 2001a). In other words, a policy of openness can triple the size of the demographic dividend the country collects. A retrospective analysis suggests that had the region been completely open between 1965 and 1985, Latin America's annual growth rate of GDP per capita would have been 0.9 percentage points higher on average. This would have doubled growth for each year, on average, during that period.[15]

A combination of weak governance and a lack of openness to trade appears to have slowed the potential growth that demographic changes might have brought to Latin America. This interaction is important. Analysis shows that the direct effect of changing age structure accounts for only 11 percent, or 0.6 percentage points, of the growth gap between Latin America and the fastest-growing East Asian economies. However, when the interactive effects of policy and demography are also taken into consideration, some 50 percent of the gap is accounted for (Bloom, Canning, Evans, et al., 1999). In

---

[14]John Williamson, the inventor of the term *Washington Consensus*, has made it clear that he believes the term has two quite different meanings. First, there is the meaning he gave the term, which involved consensus around a set of ten policy reforms that he believed were widely accepted as beneficial by economists. In the original formulation, these were fiscal discipline; a redirection of public expenditure priorities toward fields offering both high economic returns and the potential to improve income distribution, such as primary health care, primary education, and infrastructure; tax reform (to lower marginal rates and broaden the tax base); interest rate liberalization; a competitive exchange rate; trade liberalization; liberalization of FDI inflows; privatization; deregulation (in the sense of abolishing barriers to entry and exit); and secure property rights. Then there is the meaning the term has acquired: "market fundamentalism or neo-liberalism: laissez-faire, Reaganomics, let's bash the state, the markets will resolve everything." We use the term in the latter, now more common, usage (see Williamson, 1999).

[15]The growth is measured in 1985 purchasing power parity international dollars. See Summers and Heston (1991).

other words, countries in East Asia pursued a range of policies (especially trade policies that created substantial numbers of new jobs) that allowed them to take much fuller advantage of their demographic dividend. Latin America has yet to take such advantage of its population dynamics.

So while the demographic transition produces favorable conditions, it does not guarantee that an increased supply of workers will be gainfully employed. Nor does it ensure that those who wish to save will find themselves encouraged to do so. Neither can it provide institutions to reinforce health advantages or to create the educated population vital to an economy built around high-value-added activities. Latin America began its demographic transition, but was overly reliant on domestic demand and did not export vigorously. Many of its governments were corrupt, and repeated financial disasters had the effect of making saving ill-advised.[16]

There are signs of hope, however. Between 1990 and 1995, approximately 70 percent of the region opened up to the world economy, reflecting substantial policy reform. And it could have been worse, of course. With even more unsuitable policies, the baby boomers could have become a heavy burden, rather than an asset, as the unemployed acted as a drag on the economy and damaged the fabric of society. The opportunity to benefit from a dividend is not yet lost. Mortality and fertility rates are still in decline, so Latin America can still benefit—but only if its policymakers act decisively and appropriately.

MIDDLE EAST AND NORTH AFRICA

Most countries in the Middle East and North Africa (MENA) are at relatively early stages of their demographic transitions, having achieved relatively high life expectancy. Across the region, life expectancy is 65 years: the world average. Fertility rates, however, remain relatively high, and, with a regional average of more than 4 children per woman, are second only to those in sub-Saharan Africa. In 1997, for example, the average woman in Jordan would have 4.7

---

[16]Latin America ranks worse than any other region except Africa on corruption indices (Inter-American Development Bank, 2000).

babies, while the comparable figure for Egypt is 3.4 and for Yemen is 7.6 (Population Council, 2001).

The region has also seen healthy economic growth over the last two decades, and some of this is due to the growth in the working-age population. In Egypt, the demographic transition through 1990 is estimated to have accounted for one-sixth of the growth of Egypt's income per capita between 1965 and 1990 (Bloom and Canning, 1999a). Jordan's transition started earlier, and the country will see dependency ratios falling from 1.0 in 1990 to around 0.48 in 2040. This has been estimated to account for nearly half of Jordan's projected per capita growth rate (Bloom, Canning, Huzarski, et al., 2000).

However, if fertility rates do not fall, the ratio of workers to dependents will not change dramatically, and the region will see population growth without the opportunity for dramatic economic growth. Models show that the effect of fertility rates on the annual growth rate of GDP per capita is substantial: In Syria, for example, economic growth could be stimulated significantly if the ratio of working-age to total population was changed through a low fertility rate—analysis suggests an effect as great as 1.62 percentage points on the annual growth rate of GDP per capita (Bloom and Canning, 1999b).

Policy will be a significant factor in determining whether MENA countries are to enjoy the demographic dividend. Openness to global trade, as well as policies to support employment and education, can help countries to absorb the baby-boom generation of workers into productive and remunerative employment. Saudi Arabia, for example, is currently facing the prospect of mass unemployment among graduates and school-leavers. Sixty percent of the current population is under 25. Some analysts blame foreign investment trickling out of Saudi Arabia, alongside an outdated education system, which has not equipped Saudi nationals for work in a global economy. Among other factors, some blame Saudi labor laws, which discourage private companies from employing Saudis because it is extremely difficult to dismiss a Saudi national who is not doing his job.

People are naturally enterprising, provided their opportunities to work are not stifled by bureaucracy, uncompetitive environments, lack of available capital for investment, or an absence of skills. The region needs to work toward more liberal labor markets, while also investing in education and training to ensure wider access to opportunities. It will also need to encourage foreign and internal investment. If it can achieve these changes, combined with decreasing fertility, then the Middle East and North Africa could benefit from its demographic dividend; if it doesn't, it will increasingly face the problems that Saudi Arabia is struggling to resolve today.

SUB-SAHARAN AFRICA

This region has yet to experience the typical demographic transition. While mortality has declined, following the pattern in other areas (infant mortality in the region fell by 43 percent between 1960 and 2000), fertility has not (declining only 19 percent in the same period). Rather than a baby boom—where the number of births rises for a period before falling as fertility declines—this has resulted in an unprecedented population explosion, with the 1950 population expected to quadruple, to 718 million, by 2004. Dependency ratios have, unlike in all other regions of the world, correspondingly risen. Whereas most areas' working-age (15–64-year-old) population makes up 60 percent to 70 percent of the total, only 53 percent of sub-Saharan Africa's population is in this age group. Between 1965 and 1990, in the world as a whole, the working-age population grew 0.31 percentage points per year faster than the total population, whereas in sub-Saharan Africa it grew 0.08 percentage points slower than the total. With AIDS now killing off large sections of that working population and actually bringing average age down in many countries, the region has had no demographic dividend to reap.[17]

Although demographers tend to agree that sub-Saharan Africa will experience a fertility transition, there remain disputes concerning its timing, the reasons underpinning continued high fertility rates, and what the best interventions might be. As Bloom and Sachs have noted, "Africa's demographic uniqueness [over the past half century]

---

[17]In addition to its negative effect on workforce growth, adult AIDS mortality also has a negative effect on numbers of births because it has reduced the number of women of childbearing age. Although these effects operate in different directions with respect to the dependency ratio, our calculations indicate that the former effect outweighs the latter. See below, in this section's discussion of AIDS mortality data from Thailand.

... is *not* in the *level* of fertility but in the *persistence* of such a high level of fertility in the face of mortality declines" (Bloom and Sachs, 1998). High fertility has been the major component of Africa's sluggish demographic transition and a major cause of its rapid population growth. Compared with other developing regions in 1960, sub-Saharan Africa started with a slightly higher total fertility rate of 6.7 children per woman. By the mid-1990s, dramatic reductions had occurred elsewhere—to 3.0 children per woman in Latin America, 3.8 in South Central Asia, and 2.2 in East Asia. During that period, all three regions saw a surge in contraception use: The percentage of married women aged 15–49 using contraception rose from around 13 percent to 80 percent in East Asia, from 7 to 40 percent in South Asia, and from 14 to 67 percent in Latin America. The figures for sub-Saharan Africa over that time period are much less dramatic, rising from around 5 percent to just 18 percent (Goliber, 1997), with fertility falling only from 6.7 children per woman to 5.9 (United Nations, 2001). While some countries—in particular those of southern Africa (Namibia, Botswana, South Africa, and Zimbabwe) and Kenya—have achieved fertility reductions, the majority of sub-Saharan African countries still have very high fertility rates.[18]

There are various reasons for this continued high fertility. With limited financial infrastructure in rural areas offering little incentive or means to save, children are still viewed as insurance for old age. They are also a key source of labor. Furthermore, and despite medical advances, infectious disease is still widespread, particularly in rural areas, so cultural norms and policies encouraging high fertility in order to achieve desired family sizes (such as child fosterage, polygyny, and the distribution of land according to family size) are not changing much.

Africa is a continent of extremes, and in the last 30 years, it has faced a series of prolonged and debilitating wars. Wars not only kill and injure soldiers and civilians alike; they also destroy infrastructure and social structures, which in turn has a negative impact on a population's health. Life expectancy in Mozambique, for example, is now

---

[18]As Bloom and Sachs (1998) have said, "The youthful structure of Africa's population pyramid and the sluggishness of its transition to lower fertility rates indicate that African economies will be burdened by rapid population growth for several decades."

down to 38 years. We could argue, however, that the relationship between war and health runs two ways, creating a vicious spiral: Because a shorter life expectancy can lead to different perceptions of risk, it contributes to the belligerence of a population, and thus greater willingness to engage in war.

Another aspect of the problems facing sub-Saharan Africa is the virulence of infectious diseases. Despite some impressive health gains over the last century, malaria, HIV/AIDS, and tuberculosis are just three of the big killers that are not yet successfully controlled. Malaria and HIV alone currently account for 3 million to 4 million of sub-Saharan Africa's roughly 10 million annual deaths. HIV is particularly virulent in sub-Saharan Africa, where many countries have ten or more people living with HIV for each person who has already died from the disease. Between 1985 and 1995, more than 4 million sub-Saharan Africans died of AIDS. Fifteen million more deaths are expected by 2005, with 70 percent of the world's new infections and 80 percent of AIDS deaths occurring in sub-Saharan Africa alone. In December 1999, UNAIDS reported that 8.8 percent of adults in sub-Saharan Africa were HIV positive. The UN estimates that life expectancy today in sub-Saharan Africa is 7 years lower than it would be in the absence of AIDS. As a result of HIV/AIDS, the population of the 35 sub-Saharan African countries most affected will be 10 percent lower in 2015 than it otherwise would have been, despite continuing high fertility in the region (United Nations Population Division, 2001). The outcome of this is hard to predict, but the ratio of working-age adults to dependents will certainly continue to dwindle.

Furthermore, in addition to children and the elderly as dependents, many will be suffering the ravages of HIV disease in adulthood. Heterosexual sex is the dominant means of transmission, and the majority of people dying of AIDS are between 20 and 59 years of age. In other words, it is a disease that particularly hits those who should be economically productive—and threatens not only health, but also the economic stability and potential of a country (Bloom, Bloom, and River Path Associates, 2000; Bloom, Mahal, Sevilla, et al., 2001).

Data are far from adequate, but calculations made for Thailand may be instructive for understanding the potential economic effect of AIDS in sub-Saharan Africa. Thailand's ratio of working-age to total population is projected to be 0.70 in 2015 (United Nations, 2001). We estimate that cumulative AIDS deaths by that year will be about 1 million, a relatively small number because risky behaviors have declined as a result of Thailand's highly successful anti-HIV policies. At Thailand's current prevalence rate, still among the highest outside Africa at an adult rate of 2.15 percent, the impact on GDP is minimal. By contrast, if we simulate the Thai AIDS epidemic in the absence of the substantial behavioral improvements that actually occurred, AIDS deaths by 2015 could reach 10 million. In addition, if we take into account the number of children that would not have been born because of these deaths, the population would be estimated to be about 11.6 million smaller than it otherwise would have been. The net effect would be to reduce the working-age population by 9.95 million by 2015 (to 67 percent of the population). This decline could reduce the annual growth rate in per capita GDP by about 0.65 percentage points from a projected annual rate of 3.46 to 2.81 percent. As a result, the level of GDP per capita in 2015 would be $1,272 lower than its projected $8,500.

This example demonstrates that an unchecked AIDS epidemic—as some African countries are experiencing—can have a substantial effect on the growth of income per capita because it is so highly concentrated in working-age individuals.

Ill health undermines a nation at every level, and precipitates and contributes to a vicious downward development spiral. Poverty increases susceptibility to illness, itself a prime cause of poverty. High mortality and fertility rates discourage investment in human capital: A family cannot afford to spend its limited resources on only 1 or 2 children, because their survival rate is relatively low. The reduced incentive to invest in the future threatens the economy as well as the political stability of a nation. The UN Security Council recently acknowledged the seriousness of the situation when the impact of AIDS on Africa's peace and security made the agenda on January 10, 2000: the first time in over 4,000 debates that the Council had addressed a health issue. UN Secretary-General Kofi Annan has also given the issue prominence, reporting in his millennium statement that "the pandemic is destroying the economic and social fabric in the countries most affected, reversing years of declining death rates and causing dramatic rises in mortality among young adults" (United Nations, 2000, p. 28).

As long as fertility remains high and families have large numbers of children, sub-Saharan African countries are unlikely to see rising incomes or healthier and better-educated workers. Poverty, low educational attainment, and poor health outcomes across much of sub-Saharan Africa will slow fertility decline. Despite these problems, the fertility rate is expected to fall from 5.5 children per woman to 3.5 in the next 25 years (United Nations, 2001). Still, a potential virtuous spiral has inverted and there are no simple solutions for dramatically speeding a rise in incomes. There are opportunities to tackle this, however, and perhaps the most promising is that of gender: If policymakers can urgently place much more emphasis on educating and empowering African girls, who ultimately represent one of the continent's most important sources of economic and social progress, they can expect their countries to reap corollary rewards.

One other possible trend deserves mention: that of substantially increased migration from sub-Saharan Africa to Europe, discussed in some detail in Hatton and Williamson (2001). Two forces are working together to impel such migration: (a) wage rates are much higher in Europe than sub-Saharan Africa; and (b) the two regions are at totally different, but complementary, points in the demographic transition: specifically, sub-Saharan Africa has a huge percentage of young people and Europe currently has a high proportion of working-age individuals. The ratio of working-age to non–working-age individuals is reasonably constant over time when the total population of Europe and Africa are combined. However, the ratio trends upward in Africa for many decades to come, but downward in Europe after 2010. This pattern suggests, at first, that migration of workers from sub-Saharan Africa to Europe could be beneficial for the economies of both regions. In practice, European restrictions on immigration are likely to hold down the number of Africans who succeed in emigrating to Europe. Even if we make the implausibly high assumption that 1 million sub-Saharan Africans of working age moved to Europe each year from 2000 through 2024 (which would be on the order of a tenfold increase over current levels[19]), then the ratio of working-age to

---

[19]Current data are difficult to find, but the Netherlands Interdisciplinary Demographic Institute states that "annual migration from sub-Saharan Africa increased dramatically, from 15 thousand people in 1985 to 82 thousand in 1993." See Netherlands Interdisciplinary Demographic Institute (1998).

non–working-age people in Europe would still fall (from 2.02 in 1995 to 1.97 in 2025), but not by nearly as much as it would (to 1.85 in 2025) in current UN population projections.[20] That difference would matter to some extent, but more likely assumptions about the level of immigration will show that it will be difficult to significantly affect this ratio in Europe. Of course, such a scenario would have enormous cultural, economic, and political effects in sub-Saharan Africa.

EASTERN EUROPE AND THE FORMER SOVIET UNION

Patterns of fertility in Eastern Europe have historically been very different from those in the West. Fertility rates fell throughout the 20th century, with only a slight increase after World War II, quickly followed by further declines after abortion was legalized in the 1950s (seven out of every ten Russian pregnancies end in abortion, although increased contraceptive use has recently begun to push abortion rates down) (DaVanzo and Grammich, 2001). The fertility rate in Russia has fallen from 7 children per woman to 1.1 in the last 100 years (Zakharov and Ivanovna, 1996; Institut National d'Etudes Demographiques, 2000). Latvia, Bulgaria, Ukraine, Slovenia, the Russian Federation, and Czech Republic all currently figure in the ten lowest-fertility countries in the world, with rates well below replacement levels (United Nations Population Division, 2001). The 13 non-island countries with the lowest population growth rates are all found in this region, with Estonia, Georgia, Bulgaria, and Ukraine seeming likely to remain at very low rates for at least the next two decades.

Rising death rates have sped up population decline. A high level of alcohol abuse has contributed to a steep rise in cardiovascular diseases, circulatory problems, and violence, and the death rate among working-age Russian males in particular has soared. Furthermore, health systems in the region have deteriorated, leading to the spread of both old infectious diseases like tuberculosis, and new ones like HIV/AIDS. Reported HIV infection rates in Eastern Europe and the

---

[20]In the interest of simplicity, this calculation assumes that African immigrants all remain in the working ages through 2025 and that they do not bear children in Europe. Modifying either of these assumptions suggests that the age distribution benefits of African migration to Europe would be even smaller.

former Soviet Union rose by 67 percent between the end of 1999 and the end of 2000, with the number of new infections in the Russian Federation in 2000 alone almost double the total number reported in the previous 12 years (UNAIDS, 2000).

The United Nations posits that total population sizes will continue to fall for the next 50 years, despite the fact that fertility rates are projected to rise by 2025. Russia's population is projected to fall from 144 million today to 104 million in 2050, for example, and Ukraine's to drop from 50 million to 30 million over the same period (United Nations, 2001). This down-then-up pattern of fertility, coupled with heightened mortality, help explain why Eastern Europe, and Russia in particular, have experienced—and will likely continue to experience—very different demographic changes from those of other world regions. In the next 50 years, Russia will see a growth in its elderly population and a shrinkage in its working-age and youth populations (although the proportion of working-age people in the population will not decline dramatically). Health systems in the region are struggling to keep up with the illnesses affecting the population today, and as that population ages, the pressure will be even greater. In addition, if the adult death rate maintains its current high levels, the future elderly population will not grow as much as it would have otherwise. (For more details about demographics in Russia, see DaVanzo and Grammich [2001] and Bennett, Bloom, and Ivanov [1998].)

Relative to other parts of the world, Russia has had a high working age share since at least 1950. We do not have data on its age structure during the decades of its most rapid economic growth, so we cannot draw any conclusions about the relationship between its demography and its economic growth at that time. From 1950 on, however, we know that the high working-age share should have given the Soviet Union a significant economic boost. Instead, after having caught up, the country fell behind the capitalist world economically, to a greater degree than virtually anyone had anticipated. Although it is difficult to sort out causality, it is clear that the high working-age share was not translated into robust economic growth, presumably the result, at least partly, of a state-driven economy insulated from market forces. In other words, like Latin America, Russia has failed to benefit economically from its high working-age share.

Policy issues in this region are complex in light of demography. The first priority must be health. The rise in death rates needs to be reversed and governments should take urgent action to prevent the spread of HIV/AIDS via both education and condom distribution. Vulnerable groups, such as drug users and sex workers, should be targeted, with business encouraged to play a role in prevention efforts. As several companies in Africa and Thailand have shown, the private sector can play a useful role in AIDS efforts, bringing its skills to the problem and helping to ease the burden on health systems (Bloom, Mahal, and River Path Associates, 2001).

In short, the region is likely to be best served by focusing on health, social well-being, and the economy as a means of reaching long-term demographic stability and positioning itself to cope with an aging society.

Chapter Four

THE IMPORTANCE OF THE POLICY ENVIRONMENT

As the case studies show, several key policy variables influence nations' abilities to realize and exploit their "demographic dividend." This chapter explores several of these: health policies to improve public health and access to care; family planning and related reproductive health policies to help families achieve their desired size; education policies to increase access to schooling; and economic policies that promote labor-market flexibility, openness to trade, adequate credit, and savings.

HEALTH EQUALS WEALTH

Improvements in public health are at the heart of the demographic transition. Improved sanitation, immunization programs, antibiotics, and contraceptives initiate the declines in mortality that lead to declines in fertility, which together cause changes in the age distribution and size of a population.

The health story does not end there, however. In recent years, evidence is mounting that health is also a key determinant of economic performance, counter to the frequently made assumption that causation runs only from wealth to health (Bloom and Canning, 2000, 2003; Bloom, Canning, and Sevilla, 2001).[1] The World Health Organization (WHO) Commission on Macroeconomics and Health has found "substantial evidence showing that improved health of the

---

[1]See also Bloom and Canning (2001b).

population contributes to higher economic growth and poverty alleviation."[2]

If a country is to promote the demographic transition and take advantage of the demographic dividend, five health policies should be prioritized:

- First, ensuring that infants receive effective medical care is of paramount importance, as a high degree of certainty about a child's chances of survival is vital to the completion of the demographic transition. Such certainty precludes the need to have more offspring and will mean that investment in education is concentrated in fewer children.

- Second, the health of women is critical for two main reasons. Women's access to reproductive health services is important for achieving desired family sizes. Women are also essential conduits of knowledge about health: A healthier woman will likely improve the health of her family.

- Third, children need to have adequate support for their health needs in order to ensure they maximize their opportunities in the education system, where poor health often contributes to educational underachievement (Ruger, Jamison, and Bloom, 2001).

- Fourth, as the baby-boom generation enters the workforce, a proportion of the prosperity they generate will have to be channeled back into policies that improve their health. This is not an area where the market will necessarily suffice, as market failures in the public health area are pervasive, and the institutions and technologies that support health must instead be generated through efforts by the state, civil society, and families (Easterlin, 1999).

- Fifth, policies to improve health can prove a powerful weapon against social exclusion, which lessens or eliminates the contribution that certain groups make to the development of a society and to its positive demographic transition.

---

[2]Jeffrey Sachs, Chairman of the Commission, quoted in WHO South East Asia press release, April 17, 2000.

Ill health causes poverty and it keeps people in poverty, both at a family and a national level. The World Bank has reported that when households become poorer, the most common reason is illness, injury, or death (World Bank Group, 2002).

Implementation of policies to improve health is a complex process, with a range of medical, public health, and non-health interventions from which to choose. Medical interventions, such as vaccines and drugs, primary health care centers, and clinics, offer the opportunity for high-profile, cost-effective action against clearly identified health problems. So-called "vertical" interventions, such as vaccination campaigns, work best when they are conducted on a massive scale and where near-universal take-up multiplies the benefit. However, vertical interventions are currently poorly funded, and there is an overwhelming need for increased funding at an international level both for the development of new vaccines and cures, and for more effective delivery. This international public good is not being delivered by the market, with only 11 of 1,223 new drugs launched on the market between 1975 and 1997 designed to tackle tropical diseases. Potential solutions include governments receiving more assistance from international organizations such as the Global Alliance for Vaccines and Immunization, or working more constructively with the private sector to fill the breach (Economist.com, 1999).

Nonmedical interventions are aimed at working more broadly to strengthen health systems. Priorities include the need to develop better data for decisionmaking and to use these data to set priorities for decisionmaking. Ministries should aim to develop a new role that emphasizes facilitation, sponsorship of innovation, finance, and supervisory capabilities, beyond the traditional emphasis on delivery. Partnerships between the public sector, civil society, and the private sector have the potential to be fruitful, but these partnerships need leadership if they are to develop (Reich, 2000).

Health outcomes can also be improved by non-health policies and by exploiting positive feedback between different policy areas. "Virtuous spirals" are possible as, for example, educated people seek better health, while healthy people are more receptive consumers of education.

POPULATION POLICY AND THE FAMILY

Population policy has a direct impact on the speed, timing, and completion of the demographic transition, with corresponding effects on the amplitude of the demographic bulge. Although unproven, it is also plausible that a sharper transition has greater potential to lift an economy out of a poverty trap and onto a higher, steeper, and sustainable growth trajectory. This could have important policy implications, highlighting, for example, family planning as an instrument of economic growth above and beyond its contribution to reproductive health.

The Population Council estimates that at least 120 million women in developing countries have an unmet need for contraception,[3] while the United Nations Population Fund estimates that half of the world's 175 million pregnancies a year are unwanted or mistimed (Population Council, 1995; United Nations Populations Fund, 1999). In developing countries, excluding China, approximately one-fourth of all births are unwanted (Bongaarts, 1999). Research suggests that if women were to reach (but not exceed) their desired family size, this would achieve targets for fertility reduction in 13 out of 17 countries whose governments have quantitative targets to reduce fertility (Sinding, Ross, and Rosenfield, 1994). Lack of knowledge about contraceptive methods, concern about possible side effects, and the possibility of disapproval from partners and other members of the community have been identified as key factors limiting use of family planning services (Bongaarts and Bruce, 1995). The impact of family planning programs on fertility rates has been highly significant, exceeding the impact of socioeconomic factors such as rising income. It has been estimated that programs have reduced fertility by between 1 and 1.5 births per woman and accounted for roughly 40 percent of the decline in fertility in the 1960s, '70s, and '80s (Bongaarts, 1997). However, not all programs are equally effective. The most successful take advantage of latent demand for contraception and focus on lowering barriers to the take-up of services. This requires an em-

---

[3]According to the Population Council, "Women who want to prevent pregnancy but do not practice contraception are said to have an unmet need for contraception.... These include women who want to postpone childbearing as well as those who want to limit their families" (http://www.popcouncil.org/ppdb/unmetneed.html).

phasis on convenience, broad choice, and measures like social marketing that gradually overcome resistance to use of contraception (Bulatao, 1998).

Without trying to dictate the number of children couples may or should have, governments can at least put in place policies to facilitate family planning and respond to demand. Political support can help facilitate institutional change and encourage new forms of behavior. It is also vital for ensuring proper financing, especially in the critical phase where pilot programs are built on to provide near-universal coverage. As the use of contraception becomes institutionalized, however, governments may be able to withdraw, at least partially, from provision and financing, as other actors take responsibility for meeting a constant and established demand. Donor support can also facilitate progress, by establishing an international climate that encourages the research, development, and roll-out of contraceptive services; by sponsoring a political dialogue to help build a consensus about the need for effective population policy; and by supporting governments as they develop national programs. Donors can also help promote delivery standards, provide training at all levels, and help evaluate the comparative effectiveness—or ineffectiveness—of national programs (Bulatao, 1998).

Other policies can have a powerful influence on reproductive behavior and health. Education is a significant influence on family size—more-educated parents face higher opportunity costs as their families grow, and are also likely to wish to invest heavily in the education of their children. Policies to improve the socioeconomic position of women will have an impact on fertility similar to that of increasing the quantity and quality of education. Antidiscrimination legislation in the workplace and credit market, for example, will help improve women's opportunities for employment and will raise opportunity costs of having children. As women's standing increases within a household, they are also more likely to drive institutional and cultural change, which typically leads to smaller families and improved opportunities for children.

The effect of the demographic transition on women is part of a more general impact on family structures and gender relations. Smaller families, increased empowerment of women, and urbanization are also associated with rising divorce rates. Family breakdown can have highly adverse social effects. Single-parent families and single-person households have become more common across the developed world, with approximately half of American marriages now ending in divorce and the marriage rate in Sweden now only 4.5 per 1,000 inhabitants (European Commission, 2001), which is just over half the U.S. rate. Children in single-parent families are more likely to be living in poverty than those from two-parent families. Additionally, many working single mothers may find child care prohibitively expensive without the support of extended families. Social exclusion can be the result.

Policymakers in some developing countries may therefore be well advised to anticipate the time when their demographic transition has matured. In at least some cultural settings, policymakers can expect declining or low and stable fertility rates; declining rates of marriage; high but stable divorce rates; increased cohabitation, lone parenting, and out-of-wedlock childbearing; and medium to high rates of female labor force participation. By taking measures at this stage to support the development of a "new" family, they can attempt to leapfrog many of the problems that developed countries have faced.

POLICIES FOR LABOR AND FINANCIAL MARKETS, AND HUMAN CAPITAL

Having a larger, healthier, and better-educated workforce will only bear economic fruit if the extra workers can find jobs. Open economies, flexible labor forces, and modern institutions that can gain the confidence of the population and markets alike may help countries reap the potential benefit created by their demographic transition.

Openness to trade can be a key driver of economic growth, helping to significantly boost the benefits a country receives from the demographic transition (Barro, 1997; Bloom and Sachs, 1998). If Latin America's economy had been as open, as measured by the Sachs-Warner index, as East Asia's was between 1965 and 1990, it is estimated that per capita income would have reached US$4,000 instead of US$2,950, and poverty would have been substantially lower (Bloom, Canning, Evans, et al., 1999; Inter-American Development Bank, 2000). Access to world markets, backed up by export promotion, is thought by many to be an effective way to find sufficient demand for a nation's output (Sachs and Warner, 1995). However, this view has been contested on both conceptual and empirical grounds.[4]

A healthy degree of flexibility in labor markets is also vital if a country is to accommodate a burgeoning working-age population. Flexibility means that employers are able to rapidly expand and contract their businesses, to shift workers from one area of the business to another, and to raise and lower pay more easily. Flexibility also means a workforce that is able to adapt its working patterns as the business environment shifts. Flexibility can be difficult to "sell" to a workforce, as employers are commonly thought to reap the benefits while employees bear the costs, although the provision of adequate safety nets and generous retraining programs can help persuade workers to become less risk-averse.[5] Although recent history shows that designing and implementing effective programs along these lines is a challenging task in low- and middle-income countries, the incentives for proceeding in this direction are substantial. Many wealthy industrial countries have successful programs that provide a good starting point for thinking both conventionally and imaginatively along these lines. In addition, recent research suggests that the presence of social protection programs is not closely correlated with different measures of labor market flexibility (Blank, 1994).

Minimum wage policy should be especially carefully designed. If wage levels are set (and enforced) above rates that would otherwise prevail, they effectively push low-skilled workers out of the formal economy into the informal economy. They also make legitimate companies less able to compete in foreign markets. In Brazil, for instance, the minimum wage stood at 100 reales per month in May 1995, a level that exceeded actual earnings of almost 20 percent of

---

[4]See, for example, Rodrik (2001), who concludes, "Neither economic theory nor empirical evidence guarantees that deep trade liberalization will deliver higher economic growth. Economic openness and all its accouterments do not deserve the priority they typically receive in the development strategies pushed by leading multilateral organizations." For another provocative critique, see MacEwan (2001).

[5]As a recent UN Conference on Trade and Development/UN Development Programme paper on Jamaica has noted: "Policy-makers need to tread a particularly complex path as they try to deliver growth, improve Jamaica's competitiveness, help displaced workers find new jobs in more productive sectors and provide some kind of security for those who lose out" (Bloom, Mahal, King, et al., 2001).

Brazil's workers. National and subnational governments may be able to create a sustainable balance by actively involving both workers and employers in discussions about minimum wage levels.

Absorbing the baby-boom generation into productive employment is more than just a matter of labor market flexibility. Any expanding economic enterprise (from small business to large country) is hungry for capital. Investment can come from savings—by government, business, or private individuals—or from overseas development assistance or foreign direct investment. Private household savings are one of the most powerful ways of financing growth, as the East Asian experience has shown. Individual savings are, in turn, dependent on demography and longevity. People save at different points in their lives, and they save for different purposes, most notably, their retirement.

Encouraging private savings and efficiently allocating them to investment requires reform of macroeconomic policy and financial institutions. Governance affects how much a country saves and whether those savings are productively invested. Latin America provides an example of a region where savings have been low, while East Asia's much higher savings rates contributed substantially to its development. The demographic transition can encourage people to save—but only if saving seems relatively safe and reasonably profitable. In order to promote saving, governments must attempt to provide price stability, as incentives to save are higher in environments with low inflation, and they must encourage competition, transparency, and efficiency in financial institutions.

When credit is scarce, the poor generally lose out more than others. However, the past two decades have seen the development of successful new models of microfinance by the private sector, nongovernment organizations, and the state. These have demonstrated the power of widespread credit in improving the lives of people in rural areas. By targeting low-income households, and giving credit that is often collateral-free and at significantly lower interest rates than those in the informal credit market, these institutions help microenterprises develop in rural areas and provide income-generation opportunities to poorer segments of the rural population. The work of Bangladeshi economist Muhammad Yunus, and the Grameen Bank which he set up, have more than demonstrated the value of microcredit. Beginning with US$50 and 20 borrowers, Grameen expanded rapidly: It now lends over US$400 million annually to a membership base of over 2 million. The Grameen Bank concentrates on lending to women—who now make up 94 percent of its clientele. So far, almost half a million houses have been built as a result of its efforts. Meanwhile, the Grameen Bank's repayment rate of over 98 percent would be the envy of all mainstream banks—and persuasively refutes the argument that the poor are inherently high-risk borrowers. Yunus has also used the Grameen Bank to develop a range of social initiatives, including housing, sanitation, and education programs.[6]

As countries pass through the demographic transition, they have the opportunity to examine past errors and learn from them. Many developing countries have been tempted to copy institutions and practices that evolved in the industrialized countries. Yet, in the current period of global transition, this may be a misguided strategy. Not only do industrialized countries operate in mature economies that have developed over long periods, but many of them are also finding that they, too, need to reinvent their institutional base, often rooted in the 19th century, for the challenge of the 21st. There is an interesting analogy with technological progress. No one suggests that developing countries should install analog telephone systems just because developed countries have these legacies. Instead, developing countries are free to leapfrog over the old and adopt new technologies more suited to the modern world.

Another advantage for developing countries lies in the very youth of those populations. Much better positioned by their recent education and long work horizon to adapt to new and changing technology, they can bring their creativity and energy to bear. Using the youthful population to make progress in the knowledge economy is a formidable—but not insuperable—task. It will require a willingness to invest in education at all levels, including higher education, and to attempt to offer people "education for life," enabling them to retrain

---

[6]See the Grameen Bank Web site (www.grameen.org) for further information.

for fast-moving labor markets (Bloom and Cohen, 2002). Policy-makers can use the demographic dividend to begin to shift resources toward broadening access to more advanced forms of education. As fertility rates fall, demand for primary education will drop and, over time, this effect will be repeated at the secondary level. However, demand for higher education will simultaneously be rising (at least for a period of time), as those leaving secondary education consider attempting to gain more advanced qualifications (Task Force on Higher Education and Society, 2000).

Collectively, then, there are major problems to address, and no ready-made regulatory environment of proven success across many countries with which to address them. Yet some lessons can be learned from the past, and policymakers in developing countries have the opportunity to build on these. By tapping into the energy and initiative of their baby boomers, they can promote the demographic dividend of economic growth. But, in order to avoid increasing social exclusion and unrest, they must do so in a way that protects and creates opportunities for the poor during a time of major economic transition. The economic and political challenge is to devise policies and programs in both the public and private arenas that judiciously blend social protection and economic flexibility. The long-run advantages of such a blend need to be balanced against concerns about possible short-run adjustment costs.

POLICIES FOR THE FUTURE: PLANNING FOR AN OLDER POPULATION

The powerful consequences of the demographic transition are persistent and predictable. Demography provides a crystal ball that allows a policymaker to make policies for tomorrow's world, not yesterday's.

In some regions of the world, planning now for rising numbers of old people is essential. Increased life expectancy and an aging population are the final iterations of the demographic transition. As populations get older, and older people remain healthier, countries face a new set of challenges. In some countries, people over 65 can expect another 15 years of reasonably healthy life. Over time, these will be increasingly healthy years. Retirement age in most developing countries is currently between 60 and 65. With the changing structures of families, older people can easily become more isolated, financially as well as emotionally. Pension systems that were designed to support a small older population will come under increasing strain. Developed countries are likely to feel this pressure first. Spending on pensions could push Japan's budget deficit up to 20 percent of its GDP by 2030, as the country becomes the oldest in the world (Bloom, Nandakumar, and Bhawalkar, 2001). Either pension contributions will have to increase to 35 percent of salaries, or the level of pension benefits will have to decrease. Japan's pension system is particularly at risk because of the rapidity of its population aging.

Pension reform in developing countries is therefore a high priority. Pay-as-you-go pension systems, where pensions are funded from current government revenues, are likely to become increasingly difficult to sustain, and the demographic transition should hasten the worldwide trend toward fully funded pensions. Such systems come with their own problems, of course; in particular, they require countries to have a financial system developed enough to provide sufficient high-quality savings vehicles, and a government to have the ability to prudently regulate the financial institutions that will manage these funds. However, pioneering schemes, such as those found in Latin America, have opened up discussion of these issues and led to a series of new methods of pension provision (Nitsch and Schwarzer, 1996). It is worth noting that pension reform is a particularly important issue for women, who live significantly longer than men in most countries in the world. Women typically outnumber men at older ages, and the difference is large among the oldest old. At ages 60 or older, there were an estimated 81 men for every 100 women globally in 2000, and at ages 80 or older there were only 53 men for every 100 women. Female advantage in life expectancy at birth is currently around 3 years in developing countries, but may eventually reach the average difference of 8 years in developed regions.

As the demographic transition progresses, financing for health care becomes even more important, with countries undergoing an epidemiological transition where non-communicable diseases (such as diabetes, heart disease, and cancer) become predominant. These changes lead to sizable increases in health care expenditures. Data from the world's wealthy industrial countries reveal that health care expenditures per capita are roughly three times higher for the elderly than for the non-elderly. Elder care will be borne increasingly by institutions (most likely nursing homes) rather than by the family. Again, many developing countries will need to move toward systems that link an individual's benefits to his/her contributions and thus limit inequitable intergenerational transfers. Peru, for example, has created legislation to allow workers to choose between the traditional social insurance system and private insurance.

Public–private partnerships are likely to be needed in many areas of social policy, as governments alone will be unable to cope with vast demographic changes, and markets alone will leave some areas unattended. Such partnerships provide innovative ways for the public and private sector to share costs and administrative duties associated with the provision of social services. In the developed world, it is interesting to note how government is under pressure to act in a more businesslike fashion, while business (especially the large corporation) is facing increasing demands to accept more social responsibility. While government must become more efficient trustees of the taxpayers' money, business needs to explore the effects on its bottom line of a whole range of factors—from better-educated workers to improved environmental performance (Bloom, Craig, and Mitchell, 2000; Reich, 2000).

Chapter Five

CONCLUSIONS

Population neutralism, which has focused on the effects of population *growth*, has encouraged economists to neglect demography when considering the future prosperity and development of the world's countries. A focus on population *age structure*, however, offers policymakers a vital tool as they plan for and manage the changes their countries face.

For developing countries, the demographic transition offers significant opportunities—opportunities that are unlikely to recur. They must therefore act soon to implement the policy mix required to accelerate the demographic transition and make its beneficial effects more pronounced. As mortality declines, policies to facilitate family planning and push down fertility rates become especially worthwhile. Such measures will have broader collateral impacts as well: Women will have more time to work and their health will be improved.

A focus on education at all levels will prepare those in developing countries who have not yet reached working age for their future incorporation into the workforce. Practical, relevant curricula (taking into account the importance of changing technology) can give developing countries a better chance of catching up to some of the more advanced societies, many of whose education systems have problems of their own.

As they begin to realize their demographic dividend, countries will be able to continue to invest in the development process. In principle, openness to trade combined with flexible labor markets will create work opportunities for the enlarged working-age cohort.

Encouraging savings and investment via reform of financial institutions and targeting the poor with microfinance programs will give countries the resources to prepare for the future, when the boom generation passes out of the workforce.

A failure to act on these issues could have a damaging effect on future prospects, as unemployment rises, the social fabric crumbles, and rising numbers of old people begin to overwhelm available resources. Reform will be needed, and necessary reform will inevitably be controversial. The demographic transition changes society profoundly and fundamentally influences family structure, the status of women and children, and the way people work. Policymakers must comprehend the nuances of demographic changes and help develop policies that take advantage of the positive impact of such factors on economic growth.

Demography provides a clear narrative within which policies can be framed and a powerful lens through which priorities can be identified. Embracing and understanding demographic challenges must therefore be a priority for all governments, as they build the broad partnerships that will be necessary to secure change.

REFERENCES

Asian Development Bank, *Emerging Asia*, Manila, 1997.

Barro, R., *The Determinants of Economic Growth: A Cross Country Empirical Study*, Cambridge, Mass.: MIT Press, 1997.

Bennett, N. G., D. E. Bloom, and S. F. Ivanov, "The Demographic Implications of the Russian Mortality Crisis," *World Development*, November 1998, pp. 1921–1937.

Birdsall, N., A. C. Kelley, and S. W. Sinding, eds., *Population Matters: Demographic Change, Economic Growth, and Poverty in the Developing World*, Oxford University Press, 2001.

Blank, R. M., ed., *Social Protection Versus Economic Flexibility: Is There a Trade-off?* Chicago: University of Chicago Press, 1994.

Bloom, D. E., "Population Growth, Structure, and Policy: Comment," in A. Mason, T. Merrick, and R. P. Shaw, eds., *Population Economics, Demographic Transition, and Development: Research and Policy Implications*, Washington, D.C.: World Bank, 1999.

Bloom, D., and D. Canning, "From Demographic Lift to Economic Lift-off: The Case of Egypt," conference paper for Growth Beyond Stabilization: Prospects for Egypt, Egypt Center for Economic Studies, Cairo, February 3–4, 1999a.

———, "The Demographic Transition and Economic Growth in the Middle East and North Africa," conference paper for the Fourth Annual Conference of the Middle East Institute and the World Bank, April 14, 1999b.

———, "The Health and Wealth of Nations," *Science*, Vol. 287, February 18, 2000, pp. 1207–1209.

———, "Cumulative Causality, Economic Growth, and the Demographic Transition," in N. Birdsall, A. C. Kelley, and S. W. Sinding, eds., *Population Matters: Demographic Change, Economic Growth, and Poverty in the Developing World*, New York: Oxford University Press, 2001a, pp. 165–197.

———, "A New Health Opportunity," *Development*, Vol. 44, No. 1, pp. 36–43, 2001b.

———, "The Health and Poverty of Nations: From Theory to Practice," *Journal of Human Development*, March 2003, forthcoming.

Bloom, D. E., and J. Cohen, "The Unfinished Revolution: Universal Basic and Secondary Education," *Daedalus*, Summer 2002, pp. 84–95.

Bloom, D. E., and R. Freeman, "The Effects of Rapid Population Growth on Labor Supply and Employment in Developing Countries," *Population and Development Review*, September 1986, pp. 381–414.

Bloom, D. E., and R. Freeman, "Economic Development and the Timing and Components of Population Growth," *Journal of Policy Modeling*, April 1988, pp. 57–82.

Bloom, D. E., and H. Rosovsky, "Higher Education and International Development," *Current Science*, Vol. 81, No. 3, August 10, 2001, pp. 252–256.

Bloom, D. E., and J. D. Sachs, "Geography, Demography, and Economic Growth in Africa," *Brookings Papers on Economic Activity*, Vol. 2, 1998, pp. 207–273.

Bloom, D., and J. Williamson, "Demographic Transitions and Economic Miracles in Emerging Asia," *World Bank Economic Review*, Vol. 12, 1998, pp. 419–456.

Bloom, D. E., L. R. Bloom, and River Path Associates, *Business, AIDS and Africa: The Africa Competitiveness Report 2000–2001*, World

Economic Forum, Harvard Center for International Development, New York: Oxford University Press, 2000, pp. 26–37.

Bloom, D. E., D. Canning, D. K. Evans, B. S. Graham, P. Lynch, and E. E. Murphy, "Population Change and Human Development in Latin America," background paper for IPES 2000, Harvard Institute for International Development, 1999.

Bloom, D., D. Canning, and B. Graham, "Longevity and Life Cycle Savings," National Bureau of Economic Research (NBER) Working Paper 8808, February 2002.

Bloom, D. E., D. Canning, K. Huzarski, D. Levy, A. K. Nandakumar, and J. Sevilla, *Demographic Transition and Economic Opportunity: The Case of Jordan*, Bethesda, Md.: Partners for Health Reform, Abt Associates Inc., June 2002.

Bloom, D., D. Canning, and P. Malaney, "Demographic Change and Economic Growth in Asia," *Population and Development Review*, Vol. 26 (Suppl.), 2000, pp. 257–290.

Bloom, D., D. Canning, and J. Sevilla, "Labor Force Dynamics and Economic Growth," paper presented at the Summer Institute of the National Bureau of Economic Research, Labor Studies Program, August 2000.

——, "The Effect of Health on Economic Growth: Theory and Evidence," National Bureau of Economic Research (NBER) Working Paper 8587 (available at http://www.nber.org/papers/w8587), 2001.

Bloom, D. E., P. H. Craig, and P. N. Malaney, *The Quality of Life in Rural Asia*, Hong Kong: Oxford University Press, 2001.

Bloom, D. E., P. Craig, and M. Mitchell, *Public and Private Roles in Providing and Financing Social Services: Health and Education*, Tokyo: ADBI Publishing, October 2000, pp. 19–34.

Bloom, D. E., A. S. Mahal, D. King, F. Mugione, A. Henry-Lee, D. Alleyne, P. Castillo, and River Path Associates, "Jamaica: Globalisation, Liberalization and Sustainable Human Development," UNCTAD/UNDP Programme on Globalisation, Liberalization and Sustainable Human Development, February 2001.

Bloom, D., A. Mahal, and River Path Associates, *HIV/AIDS and the Private Sector: A Literature Review*, New York: American Foundation for AIDS Research, 2001.

Bloom, D., A. Mahal, J. Sevilla, and River Path Associates, "AIDS and Economics," paper prepared for Working Group 1 of the WHO Commission on Macroeconomics and Health, 2001.

Bloom, D. E., A. K. Nandakumar, and M. Bhawalkar, "The Demography of Aging in Japan and the United States," in G. B. Hedges, ed., *Aging and Health: Environment, Work and Behavior*, Harvard University Printing and Publication, 2002, pp. 29–43 (paper presented at the American Academy of Arts and Sciences, Cambridge, Mass., September 2000).

Bloom, D., River Path Associates, and K. Fang, "Social Technology and Human Health," background paper prepared for *Human Development Report 2001*, 2000.

Bongaarts, J., "The Role of Family Planning Programs in Contemporary Fertility Transitions," in G. W. Jones and J. Caldwell, eds., *The Continuing Demographic Transition*, London: Oxford University, 1997.

———, "Future Population Growth and Policy Options," in A. Mason, T. Merrick, and R. P. Shaw, eds., *Population Economics, Demographic Transition, and Development: Research and Policy Implications*, Washington, D.C.: World Bank, 1999.

Bongaarts, J., and J. Bruce, "The Causes of Unmet Need for Contraception and the Social Content of Services," *Studies in Family Planning*, Vol. 26, No. 2, 1995, pp. 57–75.

Boserup, E., *The Conditions of Agricultural Progress*, London: Allen and Unwin, 1965.

———, *Population and Technological Change: A Study of Long-Term Trends*, Chicago: University of Chicago Press, 1981.

Bulatao, R. A., *The Value of Family Planning Programs in Developing Countries*, Santa Monica, Calif.: RAND MR-978-WFHF/RF/UNFPA, 1998.

Caplow, T., L. Hicks, and B. J. Wattenberg, *The First Measured Century: An Illustrated Guide to Trends in America, 1900–2000*, Washington, D.C.: AEI Press, 2001.

Coale, A., and E. Hoover, *Population Growth and Economic Development in Low-Income Countries*, Princeton, N.J.: Princeton University Press, 1958.

DaVanzo, J., and C. Grammich, *Dire Demographics: Population Trends in the Russian Federation*, Santa Monica, Calif.: RAND MR-1273-WFHF/DLPF/RF, 2001.

Deaton, A. S., and C. H. Paxson, "The Effects of Economic and Population Growth on National Savings and Inequality," *Demography*, Vol. 34, 1997, pp. 97–114.

Department for International Development, "Poverty and the Environment," uk@earth.people, United Kingdom, 1997.

Easterlin, Richard A., "How Beneficent Is the Market? A Look at the Modern History of Mortality," *European Review of Economic History*, Vol. 3, 1999, pp. 257–294.

Easterly, W., *The Elusive Quest for Growth: Economists' Adventures and Misadventures in the Tropics*, Cambridge, Mass.: The MIT Press, 2001.

Economist.com, "Balms for the Poor," premium content available through http://www.economist.com, *Economist*, August 14, 1999.

Ehrlich, P., *The Population Bomb*, New York: Ballantine, 1968.

European Commission, *Living Conditions in Europe: Statistical Pocketbook*, 2001.

Fuchs, V., "Health Care for the Elderly: How Much? Who Will Pay for It?" *Health Affairs*, Vol. 18, No. 1, 1999.

Galor, O., and D. Weil, "From Malthusian Stagnation to Modern Growth," *American Economic Review*, Papers and Proceedings, Vol. 89, No. 2, 1999, pp. 150–154.

Goliber, T. J., *Population and Reproductive Health in Sub-Saharan Africa*, Washington, D.C.: Population Reference Bureau, 1997.

Gruber, J., and D. Wise, *An International Perspective on Policies for an Aging Society*, National Bureau of Economic Research (NBER) Working Paper 8103, January 2001.

Hatton, T. J., and J. G. Williamson, "Demographic and Economic Pressure on Emigration Out of Africa," National Bureau of Economic Research (NBER) Working Paper w8124, February 2001.

Heston, A., and R. Summers, Penn World Tables v 5.6 (data update to Heston and Summers, 1991), 1995 (available at http://www.nber.org/pub/pwt56/).

Higgins, M., "Demography, National Savings, and International Capital Flows," *International Economic Review*, Vol. 39, 1998, pp. 343–369.

Higgins, M., and J. G. Williamson, "Age Dynamics in Asia and Dependence of Foreign Capital," *Population and Development Review*, Vol. 23, 1997, pp. 261–293.

Institut National d'Etudes Demographiques, *Demographie de la Russie sur la Toile*, 2000.

Inter-American Development Bank, *Facing up to Inequality in Latin America*, Washington, D.C.: IDB, 1999.

———, *Development Beyond Economics: 2000 Report, Economic and Social Progress in Latin America*, Washington, D.C.: IDB, 2000.

International Labour Office, *Economically Active Population 1950–2010*, Geneva: International Labour Office, 1996.

Jamison, D.T., J. Wang, K. Hill, and J.-L. Londono, "Income, Mortality and Fertility in Latin America: Country-Level Performance, 1960–1990," *Revista de análisis económico*, Vol. 11, 1996, pp. 219–261.

Kelley, A., "The Population Debate in Historical Perspective: Revisionism Revised," in N. Birdsall, A. C. Kelley, and S. W. Sinding, eds., *Population Matters: Demographic Change, Economic Growth, and Poverty in the Developing World*, Oxford University Press, 2001, pp. 24–54.

Kelley, A., and R. Schmidt, "Aggregate Population and Economic Growth Correlations: The Role of the Components of Demographic Change," *Demography*, Vol. 32, 1995, pp. 543–555.

————, "Savings, Dependency, and Development," *Journal of Population Economics*, Vol. 9, 1996, pp. 365–386.

Krugman, P., "The Myth of Asia's Miracle," *Foreign Affairs*, Vol. 73, 1994, pp. 62–78.

Kuznets, S., "Population Change and Aggregate Output," in Universities–National Bureau Committee for Economic Research, *Demographic and Economic Changes in Developed Countries*, Princeton, N.J.: Princeton University Press, 1960.

————, "Population and Economic Growth," *Proceedings of the American Philosophical Society*, Vol. 111, 1967, pp. 170–193.

Lee, R., A. Mason, and T. Miller, "Life Cycle Saving and Demographic Transition: The Case of Taiwan," *Population and Development Review*, Vol. 26 (Suppl.), 2000, pp. 194–222.

Leff, N. D., "Dependency Rates and Savings Rates," *American Economic Review*, Vol. 59, 1969, pp. 886–896.

Lindh, T., and B. Malmberg, "Age Structure Effects and Growth in the OECD, 1950–1990," *Journal of Population Economics*, Vol. 12, 1999, pp. 431–449.

MacEwan, A., *Neoliberalism or Democracy? Economic Strategy, Markets, and Alternatives for the 21st Century*, London: Zed Books, 2001.

Maddison, A., *Monitoring the World Economy: 1820–1992*, Paris: OECD, 1995.

Malmberg, B., "Age Structure Effects on Economic Growth—Swedish Evidence," *Scandinavian Economic History Review*, Vol. 42, No. 3, 1994, pp. 279–295.

Malmberg, B., and T. Lindh, "Population Change and Economic Growth in the Western World, 1850–1990," Social Science History Association meeting, Pittsburgh, Pennsylvania, 2000.

Malthus, T. R., *Essay on the Principle of Population, As It Affects the Future Improvement of Society with Remarks on the Speculation of Mr. Godwin, M. Condorcet, and Other Writers*, Harmondsworth, Middlesex, UK: Penguin Classics (1982 edition), 1798.

Mankiw, N. G., D. Romer, and D. Weil, "A Contribution to the Empirics of Economic Growth," *Quarterly Journal of Economics*, 1992, pp. 407–437.

Mason, A., "An Extension of the Life-Cycle Model and Its Application to Population Growth and Aggregate Saving," East-West Institute Working Paper 4, Honolulu, 1981.

————, "National Saving Rates and Population Growth: A New Model and New Evidence," in D. G. Johnson and R. Lee, eds., *Population Growth and Economic Development: Issues and Evidence*, Madison, Wisc.: University of Wisconsin Press, 1987.

————, "Saving, Economic Growth, and Demographic Change," *Population and Development Review*, Vol. 14, No. 1, 1988, pp. 113–144.

————, ed., *Population Change and Economic Development in East Asia: Challenges Met, Opportunities Seized*, Stanford, Calif.: Stanford University Press, 2001.

McCarthy, Kevin F., *World Population Shifts: Boom or Doom?* Santa Monica, Calif.: RAND DB-308-WFHF/DLPF/RF, 2001.

Meltzer, D., *Mortality Decline, the Demographic Transition, and Economic Growth*, Ph.D. dissertation, University of Chicago, Department of Economics, December 1992.

Montgomery, M. R., M. Aruends-Kuenning, and C. Mete, "The Quantity–Quality Transition in Asia," 1999 (available at http://www.popcouncil.org/publications/wp/prd/123.html).

National Academy of Sciences, *Rapid Population Growth: Consequences and Policy Implications*, 2 vols., Baltimore, Md.: Johns Hopkins Press for the National Academy of Sciences, 1971.

National Research Council, *Population Growth and Economic Development: Policy Questions*, Washington, D.C.: National Academy Press, 1986.

Netherlands Interdisciplinary Demographic Institute, 1998, http://www.nidi.nl/research/prj30201.html.

Nitsch, M., and H. Schwarzer, "Issues in Social Protection: Recent Developments in Financing Social Security in Latin America," Discussion Paper No. 1, Geneva, Switzerland: International Labour Organization, Social Security Department, 1996 (available at http://www.ilo.org/public/english/protection/socsec/publ/discus1.htm).

Paxson, C. H., "Savings and Growth: Evidence from Micro Data," *European Economic Review*, Vol. 40, 1996, pp. 255–288.

Peterson, P. G., *Gray Dawn: How the Coming Age Wave Will Transform America—and the World*, Times Books, 2000.

Population Council, "Why Women Who Don't Want to Get Pregnant Don't Use Contraception," *Population Briefs*, Vol. 1, No. 2, June 1995.

———, "In Egypt and Morocco, Delayed Childbirth Contributes to Lower Fertility," news release, March 14, 2001.

Population Division, Department of Economic and Social Affairs, UN Secretariat, *Population Newsletter*, No. 66, December 1998.

Population Reference Bureau, *Human Population: Fundamentals of Growth, Population Growth, and Distribution*, 2001 (available at http://www.prb.org/Content/NavigationMenu/PRB/Educators/Human_Population/Population_Growth/Population_Growth.htm).

Randel, J., T. German, and D. Ewing, eds., *The Ageing and Development Report: Poverty, Independence and the World's Older People*, London: HelpAge International and Earthscan, 1999.

Reich, M. R., "Public–Private Partnerships for Public Health," *Nature Medicine*, Vol. 6, No. 6, 2000, pp. 617–620.

Rodrik, D., "Trading in Illusions," *Foreign Policy*, March–April 2001.

Ruger, J. P., D. T. Jamison, and D. E. Bloom, "Health and the Economy," in M. Merson, B. Black, and A. Mills, eds., *International*

Public Health: Diseases, Programs, Systems and Policies, New York: Aspen Publishers, 2001, pp. 617–666.

Sachs, J., and A. Warner, "Economic Reform and the Process of Global Integration," *Brookings Papers on Economic Activity*, Vol. 1, 1995, pp. 1–118.

Sachs, J. D., A. D. Mellinger, and J. L. Gallup, "The Geography of Poverty and Wealth," *Scientific American*, March 2001.

Seltzer, J., *The Origins and Evolution of Family Planning Programs in Developing Countries*, Santa Monica, Calif.: RAND MR-1276, 2002.

Sen, A., *Development as Freedom*, New York: Oxford University Press, 1999.

Shahid Ullah, M. D., and N. Chakraborty, "Factors Affecting the Use of Contraception in Bangladesh: A Multivariate Analysis," *Asia-Pacific Population Journal*, Vol. 8, No. 3, 1993, pp. 19–30.

Simon, J., *The Ultimate Resource*, Princeton, N.J.: Princeton University Press, 1981.

Sinding, S., J. A. Ross, and A. G. Rosenfield, "Seeking Common Ground: Unmet Need and Demographic Goals," in *International Family Planning Perspectives*, Vol. 20, No. 1, 1994, pp. 23–27.

Smith, A., *Inquiry into the Nature and Causes of the Wealth of Nations*, 1776.

Srinivasan, T. N., "Population Growth and Economic Development," *Journal of Policy Modeling*, Vol. 10, No. 1, Spring 1988, pp. 7–28.

Summers, R., and A. Heston, "The Penn World Tables (Mark 5): An Expanded Set of International Comparisons, 1950 –1988," *Quarterly Journal of Economics*, Vol. 106, 1991, pp. 327–368.

Task Force on Higher Education and Society, "Higher Education and Developing Countries: Peril and Promise" (available at http://www.tfhe.net/ as of January 24, 2002), World Bank/UNESCO, 2000.

Teitelbaum, M. S., and J. M. Winter, *The Fear of Population Decline*, London: Academic Press, 1985.

Turner, D., C. Giorno, A. de Serres, A. Vourc'h, and P. Richardson, "The Macroeconomic Implications of Ageing in a Global Context," OECD Working Paper AWP 1.2, 1998.

UNAIDS, "AIDS Epidemic Update," Geneva, December 2000.

United Nations, "The Determinants and Consequences of Population Trends," Department of Economic and Social Affairs, Population Studies No. 50, 2 vols., New York: United Nations, 1973.

————, "Report of the Secretary-General on the Work of the Organization," New York: United Nations, 2000.

————, "World Population Prospects: The 2000 Revision," CD-ROM, 2001.

United Nations Population Division, "World Population Prospects—The 2000 Revision Highlights," draft, New York: United Nations, February 28, 2001.

United Nations Population Fund, "6 Billion—A Time for Choices, The State of World Population," 1999.

Vanston, N., "The Economic Impacts of Ageing," *The OECD Observer*, No. 212, June/July 1998.

Wattenberg, B. J., *The Birth Dearth: What Happens When People in Free Countries Don't Have Enough Babies?* New York: Pharos Books, 1987.

Webb, S., and H. Zia, "Lower Birth Rates = Higher Savings in LDCs," *Finance and Development*, Vol. 27, 1990, pp. 12–14.

Weil, D., "The Economics of Population Aging," in M. Rosenzweig and O. Stark, eds., *Handbook of Population and Family Economics*, Elsevier Science Press, 1997.

————, "Population Growth, Dependency, and Consumption," *American Economic Review*, Papers and Proceedings, Vol. 89, No. 2, 1999, pp. 251–255.

Williamson, J., "What Should the Bank Think About the Washington Consensus?" background paper for the World Bank's World Development Report 2000, July 1999.

World Bank, *World Development Report 1997: The State in a Changing World,* Oxford University Press, 1997.

World Bank, "The 2001 World Bank World Development Indicators," CD-ROM, Washington, D.C.: World Bank, 2001.

World Bank Group, "The Voices of the Poor" (available at http://www.worldbank.org/wbp/voices/listen-findings.htm, as of January 24, 2002).

Young, A., "Lessons from the East Asian NIC's: A Contrarian View," *European Economic Review,* Vol. 38, 1994, pp. 964–973.

———, "The Tyranny of Numbers: Confronting the Statistical Realities of the East Asian Growth Experience," *Quarterly Journal of Economics,* Vol. 110, 1995, pp. 641–680.

Zakharov, S. V., and E. I. Ivanovna, "Fertility Decline and Recent Changes in Russia: On the Threshold of the Second Demographic Transition," in Julie DaVanzo, ed., *Russia's Demographic "Crisis,"* Santa Monica, Calif.: RAND CF-124, 1996, pp. 36–82.

ADDITIONAL READING

Becker, G., "An Economic Analysis of Fertility," in Universities–National Bureau Committee for Economic Research, *Demographic and Economic Changes in Developed Countries*, Princeton, N.J.: Princeton University Press, 1960, pp. 209–231.

———, *A Treatise on the Family*, Cambridge, Mass.: Harvard University Press, 1981.

Bongaarts, J., "Population Policy Options in the Developing World," *Science*, Vol. 263, 1994, pp. 771–776.

Caselli, F., G. Esquivel, and F. Lefort, "Reopening the Convergence Debate: A New Look at Cross-Country Growth Empirics," *Journal of Economic Growth*, Vol. 1, 1996, pp. 363–389.

Commission on Macroeconomics and Health, *Macroeconomics and Health: Investing in Health for Economic Development*, Geneva: World Health Organization, 2001.

Condorcet, M. J. A. N., *Sketch for a Historical Picture of the Progress of the Human Mind*, Barraclough, J., trans., London: Weidenfeld and Nicolson (1955), 1795.

Fogel, R., *Economic Growth, Population Theory, and Physiology: The Bearing of Long-Term Processes on the Making of Economic Policy*, National Bureau of Economic Research (NBER) Working Paper 4638, 1994.

————, *The Relevance of Malthus for the Study of Mortality Today: Long-Run Influences on Health, Mortality, Labour Force Participation, and Economic Growth,* National Bureau of Economic Research (NBER) Working Paper H0054, 1994.

————, "The Contribution of Improved Nutrition to the Decline in Mortality Rates in Europe and America," in Julian Simon, ed., *The State of Humanity,* Cambridge, Mass.: Blackwell Publishers, 1995.

Fukuyama, F., *The Great Disruption: Human Nature and the Reconstitution of Social Order,* New York: The Free Press, 1999.

Furedi, F., *Population and Development: A Critical Introduction,* New York: St. Martin's Press, 1997.

Godwin, W., *An Enquiry Concerning Political Justice, and Its Influence on General Virtue and Happiness,* New York: Woodstock Books (1992), 1793.

————, *Of Population,* London: J. McGowan, 1820.

Hayek, F. A., 1988. "The Fatal Conceit: The Errors of Socialism," in *The Collected Works of F. A. Hayek,* Vol. 1, Chicago: University of Chicago Press, 1988.

Hirschman, A., *The Strategy of Economic Development,* New Haven: Yale University Press, 1958.

Jones, G., *Social Hygiene in Twentieth Century Britain,* Wolfeboro, N.H.: Croom Helm, 1986.

Kelley, A., and R. Schmidt, "Economic and Demographic Change: A Synthesis of Models, Findings, and Perspectives," in N. Birdsall, A. C. Kelley, and S. W. Sinding, eds., *Population Matters: Demographic Change, Economic Growth, and Poverty in the Developing World,* Oxford University Press, 2001.

Kennedy, P., *Preparing for the Twenty-First Century,* New York: Random House, 1993.

Keynes, J. M., *The Economic Consequences of the Peace,* New York: Harcourt, Brace, 1920.

———, "Some Economic Consequences of a Declining Population," *Eugenics Review*, Vol. 29, 1937, pp. 13–17.

Lewis, W. A., *Theory of Economic Growth*, London: Allen & Unwin, 1955.

Lindh, T., and B. Malmberg, "Age Structure and Inflation: A Wicksellian Interpretation of the OECD Data," *Journal of Economic Behavior and Organization*, Vol. 36, No. 1, 1998, pp. 19–37.

———, "Age Structure and the Current Account. A Changing Relation?" Uppsala: Uppsala University, Department of Economics, 1999.

———, "Can Age Structure Forecast Inflation Trends?" *Journal of Economics and Business*, Vol. 52(1/2), 2000, pp. 31–49.

Meade, J., "Population Explosion, the Standard of Living, and Social Conflict," *Economic Journal*, Vol. 77, 1967, pp. 233–255.

Mill, J. S., *Principles of Political Economy*, New York: Oxford University Press (The World's Classics, 1994), 1848.

Myrdal, G., *Population: A Problem for Democracy*, Cambridge, Mass.: Harvard University Press, 1940.

North, D., and R. Thomas, "An Economic Theory of the Growth of the Western World," *Economic History Review*, Vol. 23, No. 1, 1970, pp. 1–17.

Paes de Barros, R., S. Firpo, R. Guedes Barreto, and P. G. Pereira Leite, "Demographic Changes and Poverty in Brazil," in N. Birdsall, A. C. Kelley, and S. W. Sinding, eds., *Population Matters: Demographic Change, Economic Growth, and Poverty in the Developing World*, Oxford University Press, 2001, pp. 296–321.

Petty, W. "Another Essay in Political Arithmetic," in C. H. Hull, ed., *The Economic Writings of Sir William Petty*, Cambridge: Cambridge University Press, (1899) 1682.

Ricardo, D., *The Principles of Political Economy and Taxation*, London: Dent, (1984) 1817.

Samuelson, P. "An Exact Consumption Loan Model of Interest With or Without the Social Contrivance of Money," *Journal of Political Economy*, Vol. 66, 1958, pp. 923–933.

————, "The Optimum Growth Rate for Population," *International Economic Review*, Vol. 16, 1975, pp. 531–538.

Schultz, T. W., "Population Effects of the Value of Human Time," *Journal of Political Economy*, Vol. 82, No. 2, 1974, pp. S2–S10. (Reprinted in *The Economics of Being Poor*, Oxford: Basil Blackwell, 1993).

Sen, A., "Population and Reasoned Agency," in K. Lindahl-Kiesling and H. Londberg, eds., *Population, Economic Development and the Environment: The Making of Our Common Future*, New York: Oxford University Press, 1994.

Simon, J., *Theory of Population and Economic Growth*, New York: Blackwell, 1986.

Solow, R., "A Contribution to the Theory of Economic Growth," *Quarterly Journal of Economics*, Vol. 70, 1956, pp. 531–538.

Spengler, J., "Was Malthus Right?" in *Population Economics: Selected Essays of Joseph Spengler*, R. Smith, F. de Vyver, and W. Allen, compilers, Durham, N.C.: Duke University Press (1972), 1966.

Stone, R. "Demographic Variables in the Economics of Education," in Ansley Coale, ed., *Economic Factors in Population Growth*, New York: John Wiley and Sons, 1976.

Willis, R., "Economic Analysis of Fertility," in K. Lindahl-Kiesling, and H. Londberg, *Population, Economic Development and the Environment: The Making of Our Common Future*, New York: Oxford University Press, 1994.

World Bank, *The East Asian Miracle*, New York: Oxford University Press, 1994.

World Health Organization, *The World Health Report 1999: Making a Difference*, Geneva.

n = note.